The Bangkok Survivor's Handbook

A *farang* expatriate's guide for establishing a home in Thailand.

Farang-- *The generic name for Westerners in Thailand, pronounced "falang."*

Expatriate -- *One who leaves their native land to live in a foreign country, an "expat."*

Robert Hein

Bangkok Survivor's Handbook
A Farang Expatriate's Guide To Living In Thailand
by Robert Hein

© January, 2003
Expat Publications

The experiences described in this book actually happened to me or credible acquaintances. They are meant to be illustrative only, since every expatriate's experience will vary.

The listing of business establishments and services in this book is derived from the opinions of Bangkok's expatriate community. It is intended as a guide to help you get started. There are no guarantees either expressed or implied.

The data concerning visa regulations, currency exchange, rent, food and transportation costs was valid at the time of printing, January 2003.

Robert Hein
6070 NE Emerson St.
Portland, OR 97218
www.dreambuilderstv.com/bangkok/index.htm

Published in Thailand by
Cosmic Publications Co., Ltd.
e-mail : cosmic@loxinfo.co.th

PREFACE

This book was written to assist those people who want to live in Thailand as an expatriate. It is not a backpacker's guide. Not that I have anything against low-budget traveling, having followed it for a few years myself before settling in Thailand, but while there are numerous books for touring Thailand there are very few that tell you how to establish a semi-permanent residency in the kingdom. It is the intent of this book to help fill that need.

There is a world of difference between visiting a foreign country as a traveler and living there as an expatriate, one who lives in a foreign country for an extended time. Here you will find the methods used by experienced expatriates to adapt to life in the kingdom. It is written for people who have had little or no experience in living abroad in general or Thailand in particular. Perhaps you have visited the kingdom for a short job assignment or a two-week vacation, fell in love with the country and wondered how difficult it would be to live there. Maybe you have never left your hometown but dream of the day when you put on your Marco Polo boots and set off to discover Asia for yourself. Perhaps, like me, you ended up in Thailand by accident.

I first visited Thailand in 1977 after working several years as a cruising yacht sailor in the South Pacific. I had completed a yacht delivery to Singapore and decided to leave the sea and do some land traveling for awhile, so I took the train to Kuala Lumpur, Malaysia where I stayed for a couple of weeks before moving on to Bukit Fraser, a golf resort located in the mountains north of the city. There, I rented a room in the home of an Indian family and spent my time playing golf and taking long walks in the jungle.

I had made no travel plans, just figured on following my instincts until the money ran out and then head for home, Hawaii. One afternoon in my host's living room I was watching a TV program about a festival that included hundreds of people in colorful costumes, and elephants decked out in gold cloth parading through the streets. The broadcast was in Malay language so I couldn't understand what was being said but the gaiety, the pageantry, the joy of the people captivated me. I had never seen anything like it.

"Where is this festival?' I asked my host.

"Siam," he said, pronouncing it "See-am."

"Where is that?" Southeast Asian geography was not my strong point and I had never heard of "See-am."

"It's the next country to the north," he answered.

"What is it like?"

"It is very cheap to live there, much cheaper than Malaysia," he said, "and the women are very beautiful."

That was enough impetus to get me mentally packing my bags and a couple of days later I began the journey to "See-am".

It took a combination of bus and train rides to get me to the Malaysian-Thai border town of Sungai Kolok where I walked across the border into Thailand and bought a train ticket to Bangkok. The train passed through rubber plantations and rice fields, weaving around the bases of towering limestone karsts where Buddhist temples perched, their golden stupas glittering in the sunlight. My senses were completely saturated by the time I arrived in Bangkok the next morning, but there was more to come.

While Singapore was extremely organized and tidy, and Kuala Lumpur seemed a tedious farm town, Bangkok pulsed with a vibrancy of life that I had never experienced, and although I'm a sensation junkie I got an overload just walking from the Hualampong Train station to the nearby Thai Sang Greet budget hotel. I fell in love with the country at first sight and spent two months on that first visit, splitting the time between Bangkok and Chiang Mai. Then the money ran out and I returned to the US — but I knew I would be back.

In 1980, I had completed another yacht delivery to Singapore and from there I took the express train to Bangkok. This time, my future wife who had been a member of the yacht's crew accompanied me. We stayed a couple of weeks in Bangkok before moving to Chiang Mai where we lived for three years, teaching English, exporting handicrafts and picking up writing and photography assignments. Next we moved to Pattaya where we bought a 35 foot catamaran for $2000 and cruised around the Gulf of Thailand for 9 months. Then we sold the boat for $6000 and returned to the US for a family visit.

In 1988 we moved back to Thailand and on our first day there, a Sunday, my wife answered an ad in the Bangkok Post for an editor wanted at a company that published guide books and in-flight magazines. A couple of weeks later she was contacted and given the position and I was signed on as a staff writer. The pay was good and included travel throughout the kingdom on assignments. Another time my wife scored the position of publications manager at a new cable TV station and I signed on as the writer for the English language promotional materials and TV guide. The job paid very well and lasted nearly three years. Later, I worked with a business consultant as a procedure writer for Thai companies while my wife accepted a position as an assistant for a refugee resettlement program. These various occupations did not always follow one after the other and at times we were unemployed or took on temporary positions as English teachers, but the low cost of living in Thailand didn't require a large bank account to see us through.

As a rule, the Thai people favor Americans. It may be a legacy of the lenient US treatment of Thailand after World War Two, but surely much of this goodwill developed during the Vietnam War years when American military personnel were stationed in the kingdom. Many Thais worked for the US during these years, learning English and becoming familiar with American customs. Whatever the reason, the result is a city that is very safe for Americans to live and work in spite of the language difficulties. Setting up your life in Bangkok is often easier, safer and always cheaper than moving into a large, US city. What's more, Bangkok offers the same modern health care, transportation and accommodations at very low costs.

For openers, there is currently an oversupply of apartments and a very suitable, fully furnished one-bedroom with air-conditioning, maid, pool, phone and other facilities can be found for around $300. Some apartments accept a month-to-month rental basis while others require a three or six month lease. Moving in fees include the first-and-last month pre-payment and a reasonable security deposit. Except for upscale rentals, there are no requirements for prospective tenants to provide a personal background report, financial references, or a favorable credit rating.

Thai food is very inexpensive, well prepared, and delicious. In addition, international restaurants are everywhere in the city when you want a change of menu, and they are also very reasonable.

One of the biggest factors that make it possible to live in Bangkok so cheaply is that you won't need to own a vehicle. Public transportation in the city is always available and inexpensive. Why own a car when the taxis are so cheap to use?

The cost for housing, food, health care, entertainment and transportation are so reasonable that many American retirees are living here. They have discovered that while their retirement funds afforded only a modest living in the US, in Thailand their income went twice as far and they could afford other needs such as elderly care services. People requiring intensive care or operations with long periods of recuperation have also found advantages in the high quality and low costs of Bangkok's medical services and hospital rooms.

For some people, the big question is "can I work there?" The answer is typically Thai, "yes and no." While most professions can only be filled by Thai citizens, there are numerous positions that need to be filled by specifically trained, English speaking foreigners, or you can go into business. Thailand has signed a Treaty of Amity with America that is very favorable to American-owned business enterprises. Many expats in Bangkok have discovered income producing opportunities to cover their living expenses, and some have done much better than that.

Living successfully in Thailand is a matter of adjusting your attitude, exploring your imagination, and keeping an open mind. It may be complicated at times, but it is rarely boring if you look at the experience as an adventure and arm yourself with plenty of patience, tolerance, and goodwill.

Keep the positive energy flowing!

Robert Hein

Contents

3

The Kingdom

Thailand is about the size of France and is roughly divided into four regions: the mountainous northern portion of the country, the semiarid plateau in the northeast, the alluvial plain of the central region, and a mix of jungle-coated mountains and valleys in the south. The country lies roughly in the center of Southeast Asia encircled by Cambodia to the east, Laos to the north, Burma to the west, and Malaysia to the south.

Unlike its neighbors, Thailand has never been colonized by a European nation although it has ceded land to the British in Malaysia and the French in Cambodia and during World War Two it was occupied by the Japanese Army. Still, through all these events it remained free of foreign domination. This legacy of independence has united the country and spared it from the internal strife that has marked the history of its neighbors.

As Thailand is central to Southeast Asia, so Bangkok is the political, cultural, commercial and industrial hub of Thailand, but it wasn't always the capital. Ayutthaya, a city sited on the Chao Phraya River 60 miles upstream from Bangkok, had reigned as the kingdom's center for more than 400 years and trading vessels from Europe, China, and India called there to load cargoes of teak, rice, gemstones and spices. This thriving capital maintained its dominance until 1767 when it was captured during a long war with Burma. The invading army leveled the city to the ground in an effort to subdue the Thais and it is recorded that out of one million inhabitants only 10,000 escaped death or enslavement at the hands of the Burmese. But during the siege the Thai commander, General Phya Taksin, managed to dismantle the palace and transport the stones along with his army's survivors 60 miles south to Thonburi, a village that had served as a customs port on a sinuous section of the Chao Phraya River. There he established the new capital.

Here, the Thais regrouped and resumed the war to drive the Burmese out of the kingdom. General Taksin was crowned king and rebuilt the palace on the site where Wat Arun stands today. He reigned for 15 years and was succeeded by Phya Chakri in 1782.

This king founded the Chakri Dynasty which has been in succession ever since. One of his first actions was to reestablish the capital at a small village across the river from Thonburi. Here he began building the new city and named it Krung Thep Maha Nakorn -- this is only the first part of its full name which contains 165 letters. Thais call the city Krung Thep which translates to "The City of Angels." Westerners use the name of the original village, Bangkok.

Since then, the kings of the Chakri Dynasty have been very instrumental in the unification of the country. They instituted the Thai alphabet, studied the Buddhist canon, revitalized Thai literature and recorded history, redefined government services and raised the educational standards. The Thai people revere their kings and the monarchy has not been threatened by revolution with the exception of a bloodless coup in 1932 that replaced the absolute monarchy with a constitutional monarchy.

The Monarchy

His Majesty King Bhumibol Adulyadej (Rama IX)

The current king has ruled since 1946 and maintains the responsibilities of caring for the health, welfare, and education of the Thai people by personally traveling throughout the country initiating public projects and providing on-site support and advice. Throughout its reign, the monarchy has demonstrated a high profile, hands-on leadership that has earned it the highest reverence among the people.

Affronts against the monarchy are the least excusable blunders a foreigner can commit and are among the few that will make every Thai angry. Any word or action that is construed as being disrespectful towards the king or the royal family is certain to cause some level of resentment.

This respect extends to anything that bears the portrait of the King including currency, coins and postal stamps. Every unit of currency bears the likeness of the king and defacing, or tearing the bills is a criminal offence. Even crumpling the bills into a wad will get you some curious looks.

Thais treat portraits of the King very respectfully. One urban myth of expatriates says that postal clerks often remove stamps from letters mailed by foreigners in order to keep the stamps. The fact is that the clerks re-attach them so that the portrait of the King is in an upright position since the stamps had been placed horizontally or upside-down.

Government

The King is the Head of State and the Armed Forces. He exercises legislative power through the Council of Ministers and judicial power through the Courts of Law. There are royal palaces in Bangkok, Chiang Mai, and Hua Hin, and although the Bangkok Palace is the site for state functions the king has recently taken residence in the Hua Hin palace on the western shore of the Gulf of Thailand, where he indulges in his favorite sport, dinghy sailing.

The National Assembly and the Senate are elected by popular vote and although political power-struggles exist they do not involve the monarchy and there is no movement to abolish the system. The king retains absolute power and acts as ultimate mediator when the political factions are disrupting or endangering the welfare of the kingdom.

Population

Thailand has around 60 million citizens and Bangkok's population is estimated to be 6.5 million. Although it has always been the largest city, its greatest growth has occurred over the past 25 years as foreign corporations established manufacturing bases around the capital where farmers and villagers migrated for employment.

Economy

The nation is a major player not only in the economies of Asia but also those of the Near East, Europe and the Americas. Sixty eight countries maintain embassies in Bangkok reflecting the diversity of the expatriate community that is established here.

Massive foreign investment coupled with the energetic Thai work force has shifted the country's economic base from 80% agricultural to one where manufacturing now accounts for nearly 30% of the Gross Domestic Product and the services industry contributes nearly 50% while agriculture has dropped to 11%.

In the early 1990s Thailand was on the fast track to becoming a new " Asian Tiger" with an economic growth rate averaging 8% for the decade up to 1997 when the Asian economic boom went bust. Then the Thai baht, which had traded at 25 to the US dollar, sunk to nearly 50 to the dollar. To its credit, the government instituted a policy of fiscal restraint but without stopping its vital infrastructure projects. The Bangkok Skytrain began service in 2000, and work is continuing on an underground subway as well as a second international airport and other public projects.

Climate

Newcomers to Bangkok often describe the yearly climate as having only two seasons, the wet and the dry -- both of them hot.

The dry season runs from November to April. Average March temperature is 95°F and the average rainfall is 1 inch. This is the northeast monsoons with clear skies and weak, variable winds.

The rainy season runs from June through October. Average June rainfall is 6.7 inches. Average September temperature is 95°F and an average rainfall is 13 inches. During this season, the southwest wind carries moisture laden clouds from the Indian Ocean that bring heavy downpours.

But the discriminating expatriate has discovered a third season, the cool season from November through February when northeast winds keep the average December temperature around 88°F with clear skies and night time temperatures as low as 60°F.

Average Rainfall and Temperature

Jan	1 in	32°C -- 90°F
Feb	1 in	34°C -- 93°F
Mar	1 in	35°C -- 85°F
Apr	1 in	36°C -- 97°F
May	7 in	34°C -- 93°F
June	6 in	33°C -- 91°F
July	6 in	32°C -- 90°F
Aug	8 in	32°C -- 90°F
Sept	13 in	32°C -- 90°F
Oct	5 in	32°C -- 90°F
Nov	2 in	31°C -- 88°F
Dec	0 in	31°C -- 88°F

Monsoons

Thailand's weather is dictated by the monsoons. These are names for wind systems, not rain, and they are regulated by the sun's location north or south of the equator.

The southwest monsoon occurs from May to October. During this period the sun heats up the Asian land mass creating a low-pressure area that is filled by the relatively cooler, high pressure air coming from the Indian Ocean. This air mass brings moisture laden clouds with it that dump their loads over Southeast Asia. These rains are not usually long lasting but occur almost daily and can deposit several inches of rain in just a few hours.

The northeast monsoon is the opposite. From November to May the sun's heat creates a low pressure area in the Indian Ocean and the relatively colder, high pressure air from the Asian land mass flows southwest to fill the low, but it carries no clouds, no rain.

The changes in the monsoons can be seen by the movement of the cloud masses. During the wet monsoon the clouds march northwards for a few months, then slow down and stop. After a few weeks they begin their retreat to the south, leaving the sky clear for the months of the dry monsoon.

Language

Thai language uses five tones as well as short and long vowel sounds to denote the meaning of a word and it takes ear training to distinguish the word being used. For example, the word *mai* can mean *new, silk, no*, or *burn* depending on the length of the vowels and whether the tone is high, low, neutral, rising, or falling. An effective way to train your ear to recognize the tones and vowel lengths is to listen to Thai language tapes and repeat the lessons aloud.

The grammar is simple since verbs are not conjugated, using only the present tense-- "yesterday I go," "today I go," "tomorrow I go" -- and nouns use only the subjective case. If you study Thai regularly for thirty minutes each day, whether you use tapes or one-on-one instruction, you could have enough vocabulary and listening skills in six months to see you through most of your daily needs.

The alphabet is written in a form of Sanskrit and has more characters than English but it is still manageable for Westerners. Like English, written words often contain letters that are not sounded when spoken. Learning to read and write the language greatly helps to learn the pronunciation and tones of the words and is best done with the books that are used to teach school children. They're everywhere, inexpensive, and effective.

The pronunciation for Thai vowels follow the scale do, re, mi, fa, so, la, ti, with "u" as in tune. But while vowels are always sounded, many Thai words are written using consonants that are not pronounced.

Rules for the spelling of Thai words in English have been established by the Royal Institute and used on street signs and official publications but many variations are found on maps, business cards, brochures, etc. Quite often the unofficial spelling is closer to the actual sound of the word. Petchbuxi is the official spelling but the -*ch* is not really pronounced in this case and Petbuxi is closer to the spoken word. When reading English spellings look for the similarities in the sound as well as the spelling. When you are trying to communicate street names with Thais, put the accent on the last syllable, if that doesn't get through, put it on the first syllable.

On one of my first excursions into the city, I became disoriented, not really lost since after an hour of wandering through the sois near the Royal Hotel, I ended up next to some government buildings shown on my map. But I didn't know where my objective was in relation to them. It's easy finding the general area where your destination is located but then it often becomes a matter of finding a soi, a sub-soi, then an alley that leads to the place you're looking for. I was standing on the sidewalk studying the map when a Thai woman walked out of a building and headed my way. She wore a government officer's uniform, a brown skirt and blouse with service ribbons pinned above the breast pocket. I'll ask her, I thought to myself.

I prepared the Thai words in my mind and when she got close I said, " Excuse me," in Thai. Then, with my dictionary in hand I launched into a convoluted, ill-pronounced query, interrupted by dictionary word searches, asking her if she knew where my destination was located.

She looked at me like I was from outer space then, without changing her expression, said in perfect English, "Sometimes I can't understand my own language. How can I help you."

On the other hand, there will be times when understanding English can be tricky. Keep in mind that "Rs" are "Ls" (*load* for *road*), and "Ls" can be pronounced as "Rs" or "Ns". The California college U.C.R.A. is one example, and Nepal is pronounced Nepan while Bill Clinton is Bin Kinton. When you want to pay your bill in a hotel or restaurant ask for the "chek bin."

To learn Thai language you can attend classes in language schools, hire a teacher for one-on-one sessions, trade English lessons for Thai lessons, or set up a home study course for yourself.

I began my Thai language lessons 20 years ago when I lived in Chiang Mai, teaching English at the American University Alumnae Language School (AUA) when one of the teachers mentioned that he was taking Thai lessons from a retired lady who had worked 10 years for the US Air Force and spoke fluent, North American English. I started with her as well and three times a week we went to her house for one hour sessions. The cost was very reasonable and she was an experienced teacher who started me on the AUA Thai Course. Since then, I have completed the course using the cassette tapes that accompany the books. I have also traded English lessons for Thai lessons but this has its caveats. Once, while talking to a street vendor I asked him how to say "shirt" in Thai. He replied "Su, su, sua." I thought, it was one of those tricky words like "hula-hula". I walked away from him, repeating "Su, su, sua" when another vendor, a friend of mine, called me over. "Khun Bob," he said, "do not learn Thai from that man, he stutters."

There are numerous dictionaries and phrase books, but I recommend the *Robertson's Practical English-Thai Dictionary*. The vocabulary is based on North American English for meanings and sounds and the words are written in English, phonetic spelling, and formal Thai. It also includes an excellent selection of useful phrases, a rare quality in dictionaries, and an easily understood method for learning to pronounce Thai words.

English-Thai dictionaries and language programs are available from Asia Books stores and the D.K. Bookstores at several locations in the city.

Thai Language Schools

American University Alumni (AUA) School
179 Rajadamri Rd.
Tel 02 650 5040
www.auathailand.com

This institution has four branches in Bangkok and eleven in the provinces. It offers a structured course of several books and accompanying audio tapes as well as classroom lessons at a very modest cost. The bulletin board often has notices from Thai students who want to trade Thai for English lessons and you can post you own notice there. The library is open to the public.

BIS Language School

Soi 33 Sukhumvit, behind Villa Market
Tel 02 258 5099
Classroom or individual instruction by native speakers.

Jentana Ngamkiaw

Tel 02 260 6138
jentana@loxinfo.co.th
In business over 18 years this method offers group or individual lessons in speaking, reading and writing in Thai. The teacher comes to your house or office.

Nisa Thai Language School

32/14-16 Yen Akart Road, Sathorn
Tel 02 671 3343
Offers Thai lessons for beginners or advanced students. Classes are held at school or in your home.

PASAA Academy

9 Soi Soonvijai 1, New Petchburi Road
Tel 02 319 2784
pasaa@Thai.com
Khun Wilat
This school has small classes and the instruction is very focused.

Siri-Pattana Thai Language School

YWCA, 13 Sathorn Tai (South) Road
Tel 02 213 1206
One-on-one or classroom instruction in speaking, reading, and writing Thai language.

Union Language School

109 CCT Building, 411 Surawong Road
Tel 02 233 4482
Inexpensive classes in speaking, reading and writing.

Religion

Although the overwhelming majority of Thais are Buddhists religious tolerance is the policy of the kingdom and minority religions are accepted without a problem. Muslims form the largest of the religious minorities and live mainly in the southern provinces. Other minority religions include Hindu, Sikh, Christian, Confucian, Taoism, and animism.

The Theravada School of Buddhism is the most dominant. This form recognizes the Buddha as the Great Teacher, not as a god. One of its most influencing features is the pursuit of the Middle Way, of avoiding extremes. This practice is apparent in the daily lives of Thai people, and has earned Thailand the reputation of "the land of smiles" since outward displays of anger are looked on as being impolite and cause the enraged person to lose face, something no Thai wants to do.

For Thais, Buddhism is not a one-day-a-week, weddings, births, and funerals religion. They practice the rituals of Buddhism and spiritualism on a daily basis, in private and in public. Practically every home and business maintains a small shrine where the spirit of Buddha, or another influential person is invited to reside. In one office where I worked was a small shrine for King Chulalongkorn who reigned from 1868 to 1910. Every morning, as soon as she entered the office, the Thai owner of the company placed a small garland of flowers at the shrine, lit a few joss sticks then meditated for five minutes in front of it with her hands pressed in a *wai*. Does it work? I've known her for years and her prosperity has increased significantly without sacrificing her peace of mind, and that, she told me, was her objective.

Spirit Houses

Whenever a plot of land is occupied by a house or business a miniature temple is mounted on a pedestal somewhere on the grounds. This is the place reserved for the spirit of the land that is being occupied. Its location is selected according to certain procedures and the dedication is officiated by monks. This is not "just in case" insurance. Thais firmly believe that spirits are part of the universe and regularly stop at spirit houses to light joss sticks, meditate for a few minutes, and leave small offerings. In one hotel, I could see the spirit house from the coffee shop and in the mornings I watched as the day shift came to work. Each person would stop at the spirit house, light a few joss sticks and pay respects to the spirit, then head for the time clock.

The Erawan Shrine at the corner of Rajadamri and Ploenchit began as a spirit house. Over the years it has gained a reputation for bringing good fortune to its supplicants and is highly regarded. The spirit house has been replaced with a large image of Erawan, the three headed elephant of Bhrama. Vendors selling joss sticks, candles and flower garlands line the nearby sidewalks. In the center of the shrine the image is surrounded by these offerings as well as numerous carvings of elephants. People pay homage to the spirit by commissioning classical Thai musicians and colorfully costumed dancers to perform at the shrine. This shrine is very popular and said to have great power to grant wishes. People walking by, and others whizzing past in a bus or car, bow their head slightly and hold a wai reverently to their lips.

Buddhist Monks

At some time in his life, almost every Thai man will become a monk and wear the saffron colored robes. He may spend several weeks, months, years or the remainder of his life in the *wat* (temple), where he lives according to 227 monastic rules, including celibacy and abstinence from alcohol. They are not allowed to work, raise food or tap their personal bank accounts. Everything they need in life must be provided through the generosity of the people.

Each morning, monks walk through the sois accompanied by temple boys carrying their alms bowls and people come out of their houses to offer them food because they "gain merit" by doing so. The temple boys hold the bowl while receiving alms from women since monks are not allowed to receive gifts directly from women.

Monks are forbidden to touch or be touched by a woman. Even when the contact is accidental it's considered as a great loss of merit. At a temple, I watched as a foreign couple had a relaxed conversation with a monk. Then something the monk said caused the woman to reach out and pat his shoulder in a "there, there, it's okay" manner. The monk's mouth dropped open in astonishment, then his face wrinkled up into a tight grimace and he quickly excused himself. The majority of monks take their vows very seriously and expect foreigners to respect them also. On the bus a woman should never sit next to a monk. When a monk boards a bus or train that has no vacant seats someone, either a man or woman, will give up their seat and women will move to avoid any contact.

Temples (Wats)

Buddhist temples and shrines are open to everyone and provide relaxing places for a break while you are cruising through the city. They are quiet, shady, and the monks are very friendly. Dress respectfully when you visit a wat, don't wear a bathing suit or go shirtless. Men may wear shorts but women must wear skirts or dresses and no sleeveless or revealing blouses. Do not sit or lean on statues of Buddha. Taking photos is permitted but use discretion and respect when posing.

My first visit to a temple occurred one Sunday morning when I took the ferry to Wat Arun, the capital's oldest wat on the Thonburi side of the river, and wandered around the quiet complex taking photos of the buildings. After awhile, a monk approached and spoke to me in English. We talked for a few minutes, the usual where are you from, do you like Thailand, have you eaten today conversation. When I said, no, he invited me to lunch so I removed my shoes and followed him into a building where monks sat on the floor, eating their last meal of the day. I was given a bowl of rice and shrimp curry, then sat on the floor and visited for a couple of hours. The monks relaxed after lunch, reading the newspaper, studying from books, or talking quietly among themselves. The temples provide an oasis of calm amidst chaos.

Wat Arun, Temple of The Dawn

Located on the west bank of the Chao Phraya River. To get there, take the cross-river ferry from Tha Tien, Tha Wanif Rd., near Wat Pho.

Established by King Taksin during the period when Thonburi was the capital. The pagoda stands 240 feet high and the panoramic view of the river and city is worth climbing the steps to the top. Viewed from the Bangkok side of the river this temple glows in the morning sunlight and displays an impressive silhouette at dusk.

Wat Pho, The Reclining Buddha

Chetuphon and Maharaj Roads. A short walk south from the Grand Palace.

One of the oldest and largest temples in Bangkok, it was founded by the early Chakri kings as a center of public education. It contains the Reclining Buddha, a gold plated image 150 feet long and 10 feet high and houses the headquarters of the Traditional Medicine Practitioners of Bangkok. Thai style massage is offered on the temple grounds.

Wat Saket, Temple of The Golden Mount

Located near the intersection of Rajadamnern Rd. and Krueng Kasem Rd.

The Golden Mount is a man-made hill, the only hump in Bangkok. The magnificent chedi crowning its summit can be seen from many parts of the city and the view from the top is worth the climb up the spiral steps. Wat Saket is sited at the bottom of the mount.

Wat Traimit, Temple of The Golden Buddha

On Traimit Rd. near Yaowarat Rd. at the eastern edge of Chinatown.

This temple contains an image of a seated Buddha, 10 feet high, weighing nearly six tons and cast in solid gold.

Chinese Temples

Lao Ben Dou Gug Temple, Taoist

In Chinatown close to Sampeng Lane and the Tha Ratchawong boat landing.

Leng Noi Yee, Chinese Buddhist

In Chinatown on Charoen Krung Road.

This ornate temple is often used by movie and television companies as a setting.

Indian Temples

Phra Sri Maha Uma Devi Temple, Hindu

On Silom Road near Pan Road

Built in the 1860s and colorfully decorated facade of Indian deities.

Sri Gurusingh Sabha, Sikh

Located off Chakraphet Road in the Pharuhat area on the western side of Chinatown.

Christian Churches

Assumption Cathedral, Catholic

On Soi Burapha near Charoen Krung Road

Christ Church, Anglican

Sathorn Nua Road and Convent Road.

Holy Redeemer, Catholic

123/19 Soi Ruam Rudi off Ploenchit Road.

Currency

The unit of Thai currency is the baht and is denoted by the letter "B" with a "/" (slash) through it. The denomination is printed in both Thai and Arabic numerals. Each denomination of bill is a different color and size. The larger the denomination the larger the bill. The denominations are 20 baht (green), 50 baht (blue), 100 baht (red), 500 baht (purple), and 1000 baht (grey). For coins, there is a 10 baht coin which is silver with a copper center, and silver 5 baht and 1 baht coins. There are also small, brass coins for 50 and 25 satang (100 satang = 1 baht). All currency bears the image of the king.

Calendar

Although Thailand has adjusted its calendar to begin a new year at the same day as Christian countries, the years are still counted as Buddhist Era (B.E.), not as Anno Domini (A.D.).

The Buddhist Era began 543 years before the Christian Era making the year 2000 A.D. into the year 2543 B.E. Both systems are used in Thailand with the postal department and government institutions adhering to the Buddhist Era dates while banks and commercial entities are dated in accordance with the Christian Era. But other than being half of a millennium ahead the Thai calendar is synchronized with the Western calendar.

Holidays

01 Jan - New Year's Day
Jan-Feb - Chinese New Year
08 Feb - Makha Bucha
06 Apr - Chakri Day
13 Apr - Songkran, Thai New Year
01 May - Labor Day
05 May - Coronation Day
06 May - Ploughing Ceremony
07 May - Wisakha Bucha
05 July - Asanha Bucha
06 July - Khao Phansa
12 Aug - Queen's Birthday
23 Oct - Chulalongkorn Day
05 Dec - King's Birthday
10 Dec - Constitution Day

Notes

19

Notes

Need To Know

The requirements for moving to Bangkok are the same as those for visiting the city on a holiday. But since you plan to live there for an extended stay, this time you will not arrive with too many clothes and not enough time.

Air Travel

Asian airlines such as JAL, Korean Air, Eva Air, China Air, Thai Air, and Singapore Air serve Bangkok more frequently than US carriers and they are cheaper. If you live in a city with a Thai or Asian community check their ethnic newspapers for travel agents. These usually offer the cheapest fares.

Although many travel agents may tell you otherwise, you can enter Thailand on a one-way air ticket, a return or ongoing air ticket is not required. This saves you from having several hundred dollars invested in an air-ticket that you may not use since you can leave the country by train or motor coach as well as by air. Furthermore, the air fares from Thailand are very competitively priced, not only to the US but Europe as well.

Money

Although proof of funds to live on is required, no one I know has ever been asked to show proof. How much money to bring depends on your life-style. You can have a comfortable standard of living for around $700 a month for rent and food.

Additional funds can be sent from the US to the Thai bank where you have an account. Ask your bank about their procedures for transferring money to Thailand. See the chapter on Banking for details.

Bank's Cashier's checks typically take a couple of weeks before they are cleared for cashing. Master Charge and VISA credit cards are widely accepted and Traveler's Checks are easily cashed.

What To Pack

I have never been asked to open my luggage when entering Thailand and have often arrived with 7-10 suitcases and boxes and stated on the Customs document that I had nothing to declare. This is not to say that it isn't done at all. You might be asked to open your luggage and some items could be taxable. I've not heard of this happening but the possibility is there. If your baggage is inspected and some of it is subject to duty, the Customs officers will hold the goods until you pay the duty. The duty fees are open to mild negotiating, depending on the disposition of the officer and the nature of the goods in question. Dutiable items sent through the mail will require you to claim them at a specified customs station in the city and pay any applicable duty before they are released.

Everything you need to setup your base is available in the city but there are a few things you may want to bring with you.

Don't pack too many clothes since you can buy them off the rack or have them tailor made for a very reasonable cost.

Bring a supply of underwear and socks. The Thai sizes are too small for most farangs and imported items are pricey.

Sport shoes in large sizes are hard to find and expensive. Custom made, leather shoes and boots can be obtained in Bangkok at very low prices.

The electrical current in Thailand is 240 volts so any US made appliances you bring will require voltage adaptors. The small, traveling-adaptors work well enough for electric shavers and hair dryers but for toasters, blenders, and other appliances that operate on 110 volts of current will need a heavy duty voltage adaptor. It is available at electric supply stores for around $10.

Sporting equipment is expensive in Thailand. Bring your tennis rackets, golf clubs, scuba gear or other specialized sports accessories.

Batteries for electronic goods are available but some are hard to find and expensive. Bring spares of any special batteries that you require.

You can bring several cameras with no Customs problems. Film is about the same price as the US.

Passport and Visa

Foreigners who reside in the kingdom are regarded as guests. No matter how long you live there you are either a Thai citizen or a guest and in order to maintain a favorable guest status you will need a valid passport, a valid visa, money, and any credentials or documents that help to establish your desirability as a guest. In many cases you can enter and remain in the country without money or credentials but you must have a valid passport and visa at all times. To be without them is to invite fines and imprisonment.

Passport Requirements

Your passport must be valid for at least six months from the date of visa issue and contain a blank visa page for the visa stamp. If necessary, renew your passport or have blank pages inserted before you arrive.

Passport Offices

In the USA

http://travel.state.gov/passport_services.html
Passport services, information and online passport application.

In Bangkok

Consular Section, US Embassy
95 Witthayu (Wireless) Rd., Bangkok 10330
Tel 02 205-4000   Fax 02 254-1171
Email Citizen Services: acsbkk@state.gov
Located opposite the main Embassy building.

When you have passport photos made it will benefit you to groom and dress appropriately since Thai consulate officers will judge your appearance on this photo. Men should wear button front shirts and not tee shirts, while women should wear modest blouses, not showing bare shoulders or arms.

Besides using it for entering or exiting the country you will need to show your passport when you cash traveler's checks, visit the Immigration offices or police stations, open a bank account, rent a hotel room, car or motorcycle, and a few other occasions. Otherwise you will rarely be required to show your passport, but Thai law requires that everyone must carry some positive identification and every visitor must show proof of a valid visa when requested by Thai authorities. You can fulfill this requirement by making photocopies of the identification and visa pages of your passport and carrying them with you.

Keep your passport in a secure place in your apartment or in the hotel safe. When you must take it keep it on your person so that it is always with you in case of accident or theft of a fanny pack, backpack or shoulder bag. The most secure place to stow it is in a money belt around your waist.

Lost Passport

You must immediately follow this procedure if your passport is lost or stolen:

1 File a report at the police station in the area where the passport was lost or stolen.

2 Take this report, in person, to the American Consulate in Bangkok and apply for a new passport.

Bring the following when you apply:

√ A copy of the original police report for a lost or stolen passport.

√ Proof of identity, driver's license or photo ID.

√ Proof of citizenship, e.g. photocopy of lost passport, expired passport, naturalization certificate. Other documents are acceptable along with proof of identity (birth certificate or sworn statement of a US citizen affirming applicant's identity, etc.).

√ Two recent 2 x 2 inch (5 x 5 cm) identical photographs, with a light, plain background.

√ A passport fee in cash or traveler's checks.

To have your visa re-stamped, go to:

Thai Immigration Bureau, Section 4 (Record & Statistics)
Subdivision 4, Immigration Bureau Room 311
Old Building, Soi Suan Phlu, South Sathorn Road
Tel. 02 287-3911 or 02 287-3101-10 Ext. 2244.

Present the following:

√ Passport or substitute document.

√ The police report.

√ A document from the US Embassy or consulate certifying the new passport.

Visa Requirements

A visa is permission, stamped into your passport, to enter the country. Currently, US citizens may arrive in Thailand and be granted a 30 day visa at the port of entry. For a longer stay you will need a two-month Tourist or three-month Non-Immigrant visa that must be obtained beforehand from a Thai consulate office outside of the kingdom. Visa applications are available from the consulate by mail or from the Thai consulate Website. The process takes two days if you submit it in person, or two weeks by mail.

Thai Consulates In The US

Royal Thai Consulate-General, Chicago

700 North Rush St. Chicago, IL 60611
Tel (312) 664 3129   Fax: (312) 664 3230
Email: thaichicago@aol.com

Royal Thai Consulate-General, Los Angeles

611 North Larchmont Blvd., 2nd Floor
Los Angeles, CA 90004
Tel (323) 962-9574   Fax: (323) 962-2128
Email: thai-la@mindspring.com
Website: www.Thai-la.net

Royal Thai Consulate-General, New York

351 East 52nd St., New York, NY 10022
Tel (212) 754 1770   Fax (212) 754 1907
Email: thainycg@aol.com

Visa Classifications

There are eight types of visas that cover various purposes and the length of stay requested, but most newcomers apply for the Tourist visa or the Non-Immigrant visa. It's better to request the special category visas after you are in the kingdom. For full details and current regulations check the Thai Embassy website at **www.Thai-la.net.**

Tourist Visa

This visa allows a 60-day stay. It is easily granted and can be extended by 30 days while in the kingdom by applying at the Thai Immigration offices in Bangkok before the visa expires.

Non-Immigrant Visa

This visa is the most important one for the long-term expat in Thailand. It is necessary in order to obtain retirement, work, business, or study visas.

Additional documentation is required for the non-immigrant visa to establish the validity of your reason for visit.

The Non-Immigrant Visa is valid for a 90-day stay unless the Consulate receives special instructions from the Immigration Bureau of Thailand. It may be extended in Thailand through the Immigration Bureau in Bangkok.

Requirements

Non-immigrant visas are granted according to the **PURPOSE** of the visit. It is usually required for anyone coming to Thailand for business, work, academic programs, family visits or retirement. Check the Thai Consulate Website for details on the special documents required.

Reason for visit

This entry is the most important one for obtaining a non-immigrant visa. Don't write that you are going to work or to look for work. This will raise a red flag. If you are being hired, your employer will assist you in obtaining the visa.

Whatever you write here must be backed up by paperwork of some kind. Before leaving the US, I obtained a business license as a retailer of imported handicrafts and included a copy with my application, stating my purpose of visit, "to research the Thai handicraft market for products exportable to the US." I was granted the visa and exported some goods and used these documents to subsequently obtain multiple-entry, non-immigrant visas.

Application For Visa

An application may be obtained from a consulate or from the Thai Consulate website. Print or type the information you enter. The application is a formal document and the data should be kept neat and accurate.

Passport

Send the actual passport with the visa application.

Two passport-type photographs

Color photos, 2" X 2", front view. Print your name on the back of each photograph. Do not use photos showing bare shoulders, plunging necklines or sleeveless shirts and blouses. Issuance of the visa is subject to the discretion of the consulate officer in charge and modest grooming counts in your favor.

Visa fees

Two-month Tourist Visa: $15.00; Three-month Non-Immigrant Visa: $20.00. No personal checks. Send only money orders or cashier's checks, payable to "ROYAL THAI CONSULATE GENERAL." If applying in person at the consulate you may pay by cash.

Application Submission

Visa applications submitted by mail must include a self-addressed stamped envelope for the return of your passport either by Certified Mail (do not affix the green label), Registered Mail, 2-day Priority Mail, or Express Mail. Metered stamps are not acceptable. You may also use courier services such as Federal Express, DHL, UPS. Since the requirements may change without notice, check the Thai Consulate web site or call the Royal Thai Consulate General for current regulations.

Double Entry Visas

When you apply for a tourist or a non-immigrant visa you can request a double-entry visa. This is essentially two visas and although you still must leave the kingdom at the end of your first visa, you need only to cross the border into Malaysia, or Laos and cross back into Thailand a few minutes later on your second visa. At the end of your second visa you must go to a consulate for a new visa. The cost is for two visas.

Duration of Visa Validity

The single-entry visa must be used within 90 days from the date of issuance. Multiple entry visas must be used within 180 days from the date issued. The validity of the visa cannot be extended.

Visa Extensions

Extensions to visas are awarded on a case by case basis and may require you to visit the Immigration Department more than once to complete the process. It's simpler to plan on leaving the country at the end of the visa and returning on a new one. You will save the costs of the extension and avoid negative entries in your passport that you have been granted extensions. Any extra entries into your passport will be noted by the consulate staff when you apply and could be factors for the consulate to deny you a visa.

Visa and Work Permit Center

The Board of Investment recently established a One-Stop Service Center for processing visas and work permits. Here, the Immigration Bureau and the Ministry of labor have combined to approve applications or renewals of retirement visas and work permits within three hours if the documents are complete. The Service Center also issues multiple re-entry permits, visa upgrades, and accepts payment of fines.

One-Stop Service Center

207 Rachadapisek Rd., 3rd Flr.
02 693-9333

Work Visas

To obtain a work visa is a multi-step process requiring numerous documents. In addition, the rules are frequently changed without notice. It's best to obtain the services of an agency that specializes in this field.

Teacher, Student Visas

For teaching and studying in private schools or private colleges, the applicant must receive approval from the Ministry of Education or the Ministry of University Affairs. The school or institution requests approval of the applicant from the Ministry of Education in Thailand. Upon acceptance, the school or college sends the approval documents to the applicant and to the Consulate.

Retirement Visas

The Retirement Visa is actually a one-year extension to a 90-day non-immigrant visa. Before applying, you must first enter the kingdom on a non-immigrant visa, then the retirement extension is attached.

This visa is obtained and renewed at the Immigration Bureau in Bangkok. It is granted to foreigners over 55 years who fulfill the requirements. It is valid for one year and may be renewed in Thailand.

If you arrive in country on a tourist visa you will need to leave and obtain a non-immigrant visa at a Thai Consulate outside of the country. But whether you arrive with a two-month tourist visa or a three-month non-immigrant visa, begin the process as soon as possible since gathering the documents can take several weeks to complete.

When your application is accepted, the Immigration Department will grant you a one-year extension, renewable yearly. This visa requires you to report your address to the nearest Thai Immigration Bureau office every 90 days. If you do not, you will be fined and possibly denied a renewal of the visa.

Requirements

√ Application form T.M.7 — obtainable from the Thai Consulate website or Immigration Bureau offices.

√ One copy of passport data pages:

> Information page with your picture
>
> Current visa page
>
> Departure card (stapled in your passport)

√ A passport valid for 18 months.

√ Two passport-size photos.

√ A marriage certificate for couples requesting visas.

√ Documents showing your current financial status or pension plan income.

√ Letter from your embassy stating that you notified them of your wish to retire in Thailand.

√ Certificate of deposit for 800,000 baht in a Thai bank or an income of not less than 65,000 baht per year. Also acceptable is a combination of these cash resources that totals 800,000 baht per annum. For example, 500,000 baht deposited and 25,000 baht a month retirement income. The certificate of deposit must be obtained on the same day that you apply for the visa and must show that the deposit came from another country.

√ A filing fee of 500 baht is required.

It usually takes one day to obtain your visa if all of your documents are in order. Currently, many of the provincial, Immigration Bureau offices have the authority to approve retirement visa extensions without referring them to Bangkok.

Early-Retirement Visa

The **One-Year Non-Immigrant "O-A"** visa is available to persons over 50 years of age.

Documents Required

√ Proof of age at time of application

√ Background check

√ Health certificate

√ A passport valid for 18 months

√ Proof annual income of $19,000 US

√ A marriage certificate for couples requesting visas.

Visa Changes and Extensions

While in Thailand, you may apply for visa extensions or a change in your visa category. Apply in person at
Thai Immigration Bureau
Section 3, Subdivision 2, Immigration Division 1
Room 201, 2nd Fl., Old Building, Immigration Bureau
Soi Suan Phlu, Sathorn Road, Bangkok 10120
Tel 02 287 3905 or 02 287 3101 Ext 2259-61

Visa Overstay

Unless it is absolutely unavoidable, do not overstay your visa. If you remain in the country after your visa has expired you could be taken directly to jail. At the very least, you will be fined for each day that you have overstayed and the violation noted in your passport. I have seen people at the Thai consulate in Penang, Malaysia who were denied visas because they had overstayed once too often. One man ranted at the consulate, "I've got to get back to Bangkok! Everything I own is there and my wife is running the beer bar alone!" In most cases you will still be able to re-enter Thailand with an "on arrival" 30-day visa, unless you are declared persona non grata and are barred from the kingdom.

You can usually clear an overstay at the airport or other border checkpoint by paying the fine. But if you are stopped by the police for any reason and found without a visa you will get a ride on a motorcycle with your hands cuffed behind your back, sandwiched between two cops. Then you will be detained in the infamous Immigration Detention Center until you can pay the fine and book passage to your home country. The fine is 200 baht per day to a maximum of 20,000 baht.

Visa Renewal

In my experience and that of others, once you have been granted a non-immigrant visa, it was renewed using the same documents. Consular offices change their visa policies without notice making them more or less difficult depending on directives from the Immigration Bureau. There are courier services in these cities that will take your passport and application to the consulate and return it to you with the visa, I suggest that you go to the consulates in person when you apply for a visa, and do not think you are wasting your time if you have to hang around for an hour. Listen carefully as the applicants before you are interviewed and you will learn the pitfalls to avoid when your turn comes.

Visa Re-Entry Permit

Let's say you are in Thailand and your visa is valid for two more months but you want to leave the country for a few days and return to Thailand. The problem is that anytime you leave Thailand your current visa is terminated and you must enter the kingdom on a new visa. That is, unless you obtain a re-entry permit before you leave Thailand that allows you to re-enter on your current visa.

WHAT YOU NEED

Airlines boarding pass (for departure at the airport)
Two color photos, passport size.
Two copies of the following passport information:
Title page (with your photo and personal data)
Visa page
Most recent entry stamp
Immigration departure card (stapled in your passport)
500 baht fee for a single re-entry, 1000 baht for multiple re-entry.

WHERE TO APPLY

You can obtain a re-entry permit at Don Muang International Airport or Phuket International Airport on the day of departure from Thailand. First you check in at the airline counter and obtain a boarding pass. Next you go to the Re-Entry Permit counter *before* you go through the Immigration Control counter. It is located on the 3rd floor of the Departure Hall, International Passenger Terminal. Allow one hour for the process.

If you are traveling by land you must apply in person at the Immigration Bureau in Bangkok located on Soi Suan Phlu near Sathorn Rd. The Re-entry Permit window is located on the ground floor. Apply in the morning and it will be completed in the afternoon.

Notes

Notes

Hualamphong Train Station

Visa Runs

When your visa expires you will need to make a visa-run to a Thai consulate outside of the country to obtain a new one. Some expats dread this exercise and many scams have been created to obtain visas without leaving Thailand, but the passport must leave the country. One recent operation involved giving your passport and visa fee, plus a commission, to an American who took it to Hawaii and presented it to the consulate for a new visa. You were not given a receipt for the passport and if anything went wrong you could find yourself in a lot of trouble. In today's world, juggling data and smuggling passports is risky business. Keep your passport in order, play by the rules of the Immigration Bureau and you will have no trouble renewing your visa. You may feel that making a trip out of the country every three months is bothersome, but I like the visa-runs. They give me a reason to travel, and stop off for a few days at Ko Samui or Phuket on the return trip.

The nearest Thai consulates are located in Malaysia at Penang Island on the west coast and Kota Bharu on the east coast, and in the Laotian capital of Vientiane across the Mekong River border in north Thailand.

Departure Notes

When you arrived in Thailand, a "departure card" was stapled to a page in your passport. Do not lose this card. It is required to be submitted to the Thai Immigration officers when you leave the kingdom.

The departure procedures from Thailand are done at the airports when you travel by plane, and at the border crossings when traveling on land.

Visas can be renewed repeatedly providing you are welcome in the country. But be aware that, upon departure, notations will be entered in your passport by the Immigration officers if you overstayed your visa, owed taxes, or bent any other of their regulations. These entries can influence the Consulate's decision to grant you a new visa.

Double entry visas

When you have a double-entry visa, you must go to a consulate at the end of the second visa. When the first visa expires you have only to cross the border, get your passport chopped into and out of a neighboring country and reenter Thailand on your second visa. This "visa turn-around" is most commonly done by taking any train or bus to the southern Thai city of Hat Yai. From there you can take a bus or shared taxi to Padang Besar, a small town on the Thai-Malaysia border. There are many travel agencies in Hat Yai where you can book this trip. At the border you will be cleared out of Thailand and entered into Malaysia. It's acceptable to immediately depart Malaysia and reenter Thailand and catch a taxi or bus back to Hat Yai for your transport to Bangkok.

If you take the International Express train you can get off at Padang Besar for the customs and immigration formalities. Then you'll have a few hours to wait for the arrival of the return train to Bangkok. This will give you a few hours to investigate the town, try the food, and watch the smugglers stashing their loads of contraband to be loaded on the Bangkok bound train.

S.E. Asian Consulates

Malaysia will grant you a three-month visa when you arrive in the country. But except for Singapore, which grants a two-week visa on arrival, the other Southeast Asian nations require that you obtain a visa before you arrive. Travel agents in Bangkok will hustle the visa for you, but their services are often pricey and you learn nothing from the experience. Unless you are strapped for time, make your own visa arrangements. Spend some time in the office if you can. Collect the brochures, ask questions and listen to any dialog between other applicants and the consulate officer. There are usually several different options on any visa application and it's important to determine which one is best for you. The consulate is not required to explain these options to you, so you must discover them on your own. Then too, dealing delicately with bureaucratic behavior and attitudes is a skill worth developing in the traveling game.

Cambodia (Kampuchea)

185 Rajadamri Rd.
Tel 02 254 6630   Fax 02 253 9859

Laos (Visa Section)

193 South Sathorn Rd.
Tel 02 287 3964

Malaysia

35 Sathorn Tai (South) Rd.
Tel 02 386 1390   Fax 02 213 2126

Burma (Myanmar)

132 Sathorn Nua (North) Road
Tel 02 236 6899   Fax 02 236 6898

Vietnam

83/1 Witthayu (Wireless) Rd.
Tel 02 251 7202   Fax 02 251 7203

Thai Consulates in S.E. Asia

The policies of consulates are not chiseled in stone and they vary not only with each other but also change over time. Keep informed by talking to other expatriates and checking the Internet news groups for Southeast Asia.

Penang, Malaysia

This consulate is user-friendly and fair but due to the large amount of applications they receive, the officers often apply the strictest interpretation of the law regarding requests for non-immigrant visas. It is located on the west coast of Malaysia and the visa-run may be made by bus, train, or air.

Kota Bharu Malaysia

This consulate is reported to be less heavy-handed than Penang. It is not on the main route between Singapore and Bangkok and receives fewer applications. It is located near the Thai border on the east coast of Malaysia and the visa-run may be made by bus, train, or air.

Kuala Lumpur, Malaysia

This consulate is a better bet than Penang for obtaining non-immigrant visas. This visa-run may be made by bus, train, or air.

Phnom Penh, Cambodia

This consulate has a very good reputation among expatriates for granting visas. The visa-run can be done by bus from the Thai border but air travel is the best.

Vientiane, Laos

This consulate has a mixed record for granting visas. This visa-run may be made by bus, train, or air.

Singapore and Hong Kong

Unless their attitudes have changed a lot, the consulates at Singapore and Hong Kong are not recommended.

Georgetown, Penang Island, Malaysia

The consulate at Georgetown has long been the favorite place for expats to make their visa-runs since it is accessible by plane, train or motor coach and the Malaysian Immigration automatically grants a no-fee, three-month visa to visitors.

By Air

When you go by air it is possible to complete the visa-run in one day. If you arrive at the Thai Consulate in Georgetown when it opens at 9 A.M. you can have your visa application approved and return to Bangkok the same afternoon. The visa processing will take a couple of hours but is completed by noon.

By Motor Coach

Motor coaches are the least expensive way to make the visa-run but keep in mind that Thais believe in reincarnation and drive accordingly. They have air-conditioning, a rest room, reclining seats, and a stewardess who serves snacks and soft drinks. They make scheduled rest stops and the journey is made as comfortable as possible. You can book your trip with travel agencies and reservations can be made one day in advance since there are frequent trips scheduled to Hat Yai. There you transfer to a Malaysian bus for the journey to the bus/train/ferry terminus at Butterworth, Malaysia.

By Train

Although slower and pricier than motor coaches, trains are the safest and most comfortable method of making visa-runs. They provide air-conditioned first-class compartments, second-class berth/seating cars, and third-class seating cars (hard seats, no air-conditioning). Inexpensive, freshly prepared meals are available in the dining car or delivered to your seat. Security is very good and with precautions, theft is not a problem.

Ticketing

You can purchase tickets from the Advanced Booking Window at the Hualamphong Station in Bangkok or at the Travel agency listed here:

Hatsiam Travel
866 Ploenchit Rd. at Wireless Rd. intersection
Tel 02 255 5420-27 Fax 02 253 7978
hatsiam_Thailand@hotmail.com
Train, tickets, Songserm Travel agent

Online Reservations

Website: State Railway of Thailand
www.thailandrailway.com

Go to website and Click on the SERVICES button. On the SERVICES page are listed the TYPES OF CARS, TIMETABLE, and RATE OF CHARGE (fare). The fare will require some figuring out since there are supplemental charges due depending on the class of seat you book.

Determine the type of car you want, then go to the TIMETABLE and choose SOUTHERN LINE ARRIVALS AND DEPARTURES. This will install the Adobe Acrobat reader and display the daily schedule of trains to and from Bangkok.

At the top of each column is an identification number of the train. When I last checked, the number for the Bangkok to Butterworth express train was 36. But it is subject to change.

Send an email to **passenger-ser@srt.or.th** with the following information:

√   The class of car you want

√   The identification number of the train

√   The date you want to depart

You will receive an email confirmation of your reservations but you will have to purchase your ticket from the Advance Booking window at the Hualamphong Train Station. Purchase your ticket at least one week before departure.

To book a berth on the International Express you must make reservations a few weeks in advance. It's advisable to make your return-trip reservations at the same time.

Return Reservations

It is possible to return to Bangkok on the day after you arrive in Georgetown. Say you leave Bangkok on Sunday, arrive in Georgetown and submit your visa application on Monday afternoon, then collect your passport and visa on Tuesday morning and board the train for Bangkok on Tuesday afternoon and arrive in Bangkok on Wednesday morning. But you must be aware of the days when the consulate is closed and schedule your return trip accordingly. Fortunately, if you must remain in Georgetown for a few days, the rent and food are inexpensive.

The train leaves Bangkok's Hualamphong Station each afternoon at 3:15 P.M. and arrives at the train/bus/ferry terminal in Butterworth, Malaysia around noon the next day. From there, it's a short walk to the dock where you board a ferry to Georgetown, the capital of Penang Island, a mile offshore.

At Georgetown, Penang Island

From the Georgetown landing you can take a taxi or a bus to the Thai consulate on Jalan Nunn just off of Jalan Macalister. The taxi fares are around $3. There are always other visa-runners on the ferry and it's common to share a taxi. Ask around.

Across the street from the landing is a bus depot where you can catch a No. 7 bus to the consulate. The conductors speak English and will tell you where to get off. The buses run every 30 minutes.

The Thai Consulate is open Monday through Friday (except for Thai or Malaysian holidays) from 9 A.M. to noon and again from 1 P.M. to 3 P.M. If you submit your visa application when the Consulate opens at 9 A.M. you will receive your visa before noon. If you submit your application between 1 and 3 P.M. you will be told to come back the next day at 11 A.M. to collect your passport, unless you apply on Friday or the day before a Thai or Malaysian holiday. Two passport pictures are required and the visa fee may be paid in either Thai or Malaysian currency.

Alternatively, you could check into a hotel as soon as you get off the ferry and have the hotel's courier services deliver your passport and visa application to the consulate and pick it up the next day for you. All the hotels offer this service, but they have been known to stall in order to keep you as a guest for an extra day. Although this service saves you the errand it could be a problem if the courier is involved in an accident on his motorbike, scattering passports on the street.

I like going to the consulate. It's a small office and I overhear conversations between the officers and applicants as rules are explained. More than once those discussions showed me how to fill out my application in order to get the best visa possible.

Georgetown Accommodations

Now you can look for your accommodations. Georgetown has dozens of hotels ranging from backpacker-budget to luxury, and a clean, secure room can be found for less than $20. Chulia Street is the main drag for budget travelers. It's near the ferry landing and lined with hotels and restaurants.

The E&O Hotel is a fascinating, and reasonable, establishment from the British colonial period.

Return to Bangkok

The train to Bangkok departs Butterworth at 1:40 P.M. and visas can be picked up at the Thai consulate early enough to catch the train.

Train tickets from Butterworth to Bangkok can be obtained from the Malaysian Railway counter at the ferry terminal in Penang but you can not pre-book a sleeper car from there. If you want to ensure that you have a sleeper car back to Bangkok, buy your return tickets and make firm reservations when you book your trip in Bangkok. Plan the return trip carefully, since it will cost you a fee to cancel your reservations.

The train for Bangkok leaves Butterworth with a mix of first, second, and third-class cars. In Hat Yai, at least five more cars including a restaurant car are added to the train. You can not pre-book these cars from Malaysia.

As a rule, the second-class sleeper cars are fully booked a week in advance and the only tickets available are for standard second-class and third-class seats.

But there are always "no-shows" for the air-conditioned, second-class cars. Tell your conductor that you would like to upgrade your seat and to notify you of a vacancy.

Kota Bharu, Malaysia

Kota Bharu, on the east coast of Malaysia also has a Thai Consulate. It is a very quiet little town, the cost of living is reasonable and there are plenty of places to stay. This consulate may be slightly more lenient than the one in Penang with a better chance for upgrading your visa to non-immigrant or to obtain multiple-entry visas.

Take an overnight train from Bangkok Hualamphong Station to Sungai Kolok, a town on the southeastern Thai-Malaysia border. Make reservations a couple of weeks in advance if you want a sleeper berth.

A motorcycle taxi will take you to the border for 20 baht. There you cross out of Thailand, into Malaysia and take a taxi or bus for the two-hour journey to Kota Bharu. The Thai Consulate is only a short taxi ride from guest houses and hotels.

Vientiane, Laos

A visa-run to Vientiane, Laos requires a Laotian visa. This can be obtained from the Laotian Consulate and travel agents in Bangkok or at the border crossing in Nong Khai. The cost is around $30-40.

Take the northbound train to Nong Khai that departs from Hualamphong Station around 8 P.M. A sleeper car is advisable since it is an overnight journey to the Thai border town of Nong Khai on the Mekong River. There you go through the departure procedure from Thailand and cross the Friendship Bridge into Laos. From there, the trip into Vientiane by tuk-tuk, about 9 miles, costs 100-150 baht. The visa process takes 2 working days. Don't forget to include two passport photos with your application.

The Penang Consulate

Notes

45

Notes

Arriving at Bangkok

47

For a layout of the arrival area, go to the website for the Airport Authority of Thailand, **www.airportthai.or.th.** Click on the Bangkok International Airport icon.

Bangkok is one of the softest landing spots in Asia for Immigration and Customs formalities. Upon arrival at Don Muang Airport, the first stop you will make is the Immigration Counter where your visa will be stamped and a Departure Card stapled into your passport. Don't lose this card since you will need it to leave the kingdom.

Next, you collect your baggage and to the Customs Inspection station. What happens here varies from person to person for although the Customs Regulations are clearly written, interpretation and enforcement are ultimately in the control of the inspector at the gate. Over the years I have made numerous trips into the kingdom and except to ensure that I had the correct claim tickets, I have never had my baggage inspected. This includes times when I arrived with several carts loaded with suitcases and cartons. I was simply waved through. In addition, none of my expat friends have ever been through a baggage check. That's not to say that it doesn't happen. If you get an inspector who is applying the letter of the law and finds that you brought more than the quota of tobacco or liquor you will be asked to pay duty on these goods before they are released. I always claim "nothing to declare" on the customs declaration card and have never been questioned.

Into The City

After clearing Customs you enter a large waiting room. Go to the money exchange counter to change dollars into Thai baht. Be sure to obtain several bills of 20, 50 and 100 baht denominations.

If you have reserved a hotel room there may be airport pickup included or you can inquire at the information desk about a coach service that goes there. If you haven't booked your accommodations, take a taxi that will stay with you until you find a room. The options available depend on what time you arrive.

Many of the flights from the USA arrive after midnight when the coach service is closed and you'll have to take a taxi. In the arrivals foyer there are several taxi-booking desks. The fare is around 650 baht.

You have more options when you arrive in the daytime or early evening hours. Besides taxis, there are motor coaches that call at several hotels and a special Airport Bus, with space for luggage, that goes directly to Sukhumvit Road. Or you can walk out of the airport to Vipavadee Rangsit Road where you can catch an air-conditioned city bus or hail a taxi. If you are on a very tight budget, you can cross the pedestrian overpass from the airport to the train station where, for about 50 cents, you can take the train to Hualamphong, the main station in Bangkok. There you will find buses that go to most areas of the city. I've used all these methods depending on what time I arrive, how much luggage I have and where I'm going, but one thing I don't do is take a free-lance taxi from the airport. These are non-metered and often unmarked "taxis" that cruise around hustling fares. Not only are the cabs in poor condition but quite often so is the driver. For me, that's putting too much trust in my "what-goes-around-comes-around" karma.

Sukhumvit Base

For decades, the Sukhumvit area has been a favorite place for expatriates living in Bangkok. It has scores of apartments, restaurants, shopping centers, banks and hospitals where English is spoken. It also provides good transportation links to all sections of the city.

Sukhumvit Road is actually a continuation of Ploenchit Road and Rama I Road and is a main boulevard in Thailand. It begins where the expressway and train tracks cross over Ploenchit Road near the Wireless Road intersection and heads southeast for a few miles before turning due south out of the city and on to the cities of Chonburi, Pattaya, and Sattahip on the eastern shore of the Gulf of Thailand. It then turns east and continues on to Rayong, Chantaburi, and Trat near the border with Kampuchea.

But when city-dwelling *farangs* (Westerners) refer to Sukhumvit Road they usually mean the area between Soi 1, where the road begins, and Soi 63. Sois are side streets branching off the main road and are numbered with the odd numbers on the north side of the street and the even numbers on the south side.

This area has a relatively large farang population, both residents and tourists, and many hotels, restaurants, hospitals, department stores, book shops, shoemakers, tailors, night spots, banks and currency exchange booths have been established to serve them. It's not difficult to find someone who speaks English.

The Skytrain and city buses run along the street to most of the locations in Bangkok and it's a rare taxi driver who doesn't know where Sukhumvit Road is located. The road bustles with life and is very safe to walk around, day or night.

Sukhumvit Hotels

Sukhumvit Road has dozens of hotels and guest houses within a short walk of each other, with rates starting at $12 a night. Here a satisfactory, air-conditioned room can be found for around $30.

Budget Hotels

www.hotelthailand.com

For a list of Bangkok hotels with rates from $10 to $50. Go to the Website home page and click BANGKOK.

You will usually get better rates at the desk than if you book in advance through a travel agent or online at the hotel website.

Most hotels have a swimming pool and some, the Nana and Ambassador for example, include a buffet breakfast with the room. This sweetens the deal for you with fresh fruit, juices, sweet rolls, with a choice of Thai or Western fare, and the coffee is limitless. The following hotel listing ranges between $12 US and $24 US.

Euro Park Hotel

27 Soi 1, Sukhumvit Rd.
Tel 02 254 1074   Fax 02 254 1076
europark@a-net.net.th
Coffee shop , pool, business center (near Bumrungrad Hospital)

Nana Hotel

4 Soi 2 (Nana Tai), Sukhumvit Rd.
Tel 02 656 8235,   Fax 02 255 1769
nanabkk@nanahotel.co.th
www.nanahotel.co.th

Priemier Travelodge

170 Soi 8, Sukhumvit Rd.
Tel 02 251 3031   Fax 02 253 3195
premierlodge@yahoo.com

Stable Lodge

39 Soi 8, Sukhumvit Rd.
Tel 02 653 0017   Fax 02 253 5125
hotel@stablelodge.com
www.stablelodge.com

President Inn

155/14 Soi 11/1, Sukhumvit Rd.
Tel 02 255 4250   Fax 02 255 4235
presidentinn@cv100.com
www.cv100.com

Comfort Lodge

153/11 Soi 11, Sukhumvit Rd.
Tel 02 251 9250   Fax 02 254 3562
comfort@ksc.th.com

Business Inn

155/4-5 Soi 11, Sukhumvit Rd.
Tel. 02 254 7981   Fax 02 255 7159
awbusinn@asiaaccess.net.th

Ruamchit Travelodge

11/1 Soi 11, Sukhumvit Rd.
Tel 02 653 1314   Fax 02 653 1318
rcbangkok@hotmail.com

Federal Hotel

27. Soi 11, Sukhumvit Rd.
Tel 02 253 5332
federalhotel@hotmail.com

Ambassador Hotel

171 Soi 11-15, Sukhumvit Rd.
Tel 02 254 0444
amb@loxinfo.co.th
www.amtel.co.th

Miami Hotel

2 Soi 13, Sukhumvit Rd.
Tel 02 253 0369
miamihtl@asianaccess.net.th

Honey

31 Soi 19, Sukhumvit Rd.
Tel 02 253 0646
honeyho@ksc.th.com

Food on Sukhumvit

Most hotels offer American and European style meals either ala carte or buffet. On the sois are English, German, Danish, Scandinavian, Italian, Middle Eastern, Chinese and vegetarian restaurants that offer full meals for $3-5.

Soi 4, (Soi Nana Tai) has many European restaurants and Soi 3 (Soi Nana Nua) has several middle eastern restaurants. American restaurants are on Sukhumvit between Soi 3 and Soi 19.

Food carts are everywhere. These mobile kitchens serve fried rice dishes and noodle soups. Thai omelettes served on a bed of rice are a safe bet and very delicious. Prices run less than a dollar.

Suda Restaurant

6-6/1 Soi 14, Sukhumvit Rd.
A favorite with farangs. Offers all thai and vegetarian meals.

Tops Food Court

Soi 17, Sukhumvit Rd.
Located in the basement of Robinsons department store it offers a wide variety of pre-cooked curries and soups.

Foodland

Soi 5, Sukhumvit Rd.
In-store food counter serves light meals.

Thai Meals

These dishes are made by most restaurants and street vendors. The word for rice is khao (rhymes with cow).

Curry Dishes

Gang Mat Sa Man -- beef or chicken curry with potato.
Gang Ga Ri -- A mild Indian type curry with chicken, beef or lamb and potatoes, tomatoes, onions.
Gang Keow Wan — Classic Thai curry, green and slightly sweet, with chicken, beef, pork, or shrimp.

Soups

Gang Chued — A mild flavor clear soup made of vegetables and chicken, shrimp, fish balls or pork.

Tom Yam — A hot and spicy Thai style soup with chicken, fish or seafood.

Gang Liang — a typical Thai soup with vegetables.

Egg dishes

Khai Tom — hard boiled eggs.

Khai Luak — soft boiled eggs.

Khai Dao — fried eggs.

Khai Jiew sai moo — omelette with chopped pork.

Khai Yad Sai moo — omelette filled with chopped pork, onions, sugar peas.

Khai Pha Lo — hard boiled eggs in brown broth.

Fried dishes

Khao Phad — fried rice with pork, chicken, seafood.

Phad Phak — fried vegetables with pork, chicken, or seafood.

Phad Priew Wan — sweet/sour fried vegetables with pork, chicken or seafood.

Phad Nua Nam Man Hoi — fried beef with oyster sauce and spring onion.

Gai Phad Prik — fried chicken and chilies.

Mi Krob — crisp noodles with meat, shrimp, vegetables.

Mi Krob Rad Naa — crisp noodles and gravy with meat and vegetables.

Coffee Shops

The international presence in Bangkok shows up clearly in the variety of pastries and coffee available here. The Sukhumvit area has dozens of coffee shops that are the favorite meeting places for the farangs who live or work nearby. Here is a list of the most popular ones.

Business Inn

Soi 11 Sukhumvit

Fresh brewed coffee, American breakfasts, and extensive Thai menu.

Starbuck's

Sukhumvit Rd. near Soi 33
Sukhumvit Rd. at the corner of Soi 5.

Times Square Espresso

Times Square building near Sukhumvit Soi 12
Located in a large, air-conditioned atrium.

Tipping

Tipping for food services is not required but it is customary to leave a tip for the waiter. Many restaurants include a 10% service charge onto the bill that takes the place of the tip. But if you intend to frequent a place it's a good idea to leave a tip for the waiter. It really helps to improve the service.

In addition, tipping is not required for taxis, hotel clerks, room service or any other kind of personal services but a tip goes a long way to improve the attitude of the service personnel.

Notes

56

Getting Around The City

The metropolis is sited on both sides of the Chao Phraya River which flows from north to south. Bangkok is on the east bank opposite Thonburi on the west bank. Until the 1950s the city was laced with *klongs* (canals) that provided the early transportation routes through the city to the river. Most of the klongs in Bangkok have been turned into roads but Thonburi still has dozens of them where boats are used as taxis.

The city's maze of boulevards, avenues, streets, lanes and alleyways seems chaotic to anyone who is used to cities laid out in a grid pattern. Some major roads change their names along their route and sois (side streets) often include sharp, right and left turns along their way since they were established on private land unrestricted by city planning codes. What's more, the numbering system of the sois and house addresses differs considerably from western methods. You may know where you are in Bangkok, but the soi could lose its way.

The Bangkok Bus Map includes only the major roads and sois, but there are other maps and tourist guides available that provide more details of the small sois and their branches (sub-sois). In addition, many businesses print a mini-map on the back of their business cards and brochures showing their location.

The English spelling of street names is not consistent. The official spelling is used on street signs but maps, business cards, brochures and other English publications often use different spellings. For example, Soi Ekamai, Aekkamai, or Aekamai are the same street spelled three different ways. But although the spelling has changed, the sound has not.

Some roads change names along the way. For example, when you are heading west along Sukhumvit Road it changes names at the Wireless Road intersection and becomes Ploenchit Road. A half mile farther west at the Rajadamri Road intersection it becomes Rama I. As New Petchburi Road heads west it changes names to Petchburi Road, then to Phitsanulok Road. Rachada Road heads north from Rama IV Road and changes names to Soi Asoke, then to Rachada Pisek Road.

Street addresses quite often do not run in sequence since plots of land were given addresses when they were incorporated into the city. Several addresses may run consecutively, say 5, 6, 7, then the next sequence is numbered 1, 2, 3 because it was incorporated first.

This confusion can be very frustrating unless you adopt an attitude of adventure and develop methods for comfortably exploring the city. Inner-city transportation costs are very reasonable and, other than traffic, the streets are safe. Don't be shy about asking for directions.

If you become lost, you will eventually find someone who can help you. When pronouncing street names to Thais, put the accent on the last syllable. If that gets a puzzled look try again with the accent on the first syllable.

City Traveling Tips

Spend the first couple of days getting over jet lag and exploring the city with short excursions from your hotel. The Southeast Asian weather will be the most noticeable feature for newcomers from North America. Those from small cities or towns might be intimidated by the pace of activity, and those from large cities will be amazed that so many people actually walk on the streets and ride public transportation. Those who, when at home, wouldn't walk two blocks to their destination may find themselves part of the pedestrian throngs. It's quite often faster than trying to figure out what bus to take and where to get off, or trying to give directions to a taxi driver.

√ After showering, dust yourself liberally with St. Luke's Prickly Heat Powder. It really does help to keep you cool and comfortable. It's available in markets and pharmacies.

√ Wear clothing that will help to keep you clean, cool and free of mosquito bites.

√ Carry a shoulder bag , one with a wide strap is best. Wear it with the strap across your chest to keep it from sliding off and leave your hands free. Keep it in front of you, not on the side or in back, when in crowds or on buses.

√ When you take taxis or busses, have someone write your destination in Thai and take a business card from your hotel with the address in Thai. When you are settled in an apartment, have personal name and address cards printed in English on one side and in Thai on the other.

√ Present your personal cards when you meet with Thais in a formal or business situation.

√ Carry a note book, a Robertson's English-Thai dictionary, a Bangkok bus map, and a Skytrain map.

√ Note the bus numbers that pass by your hotel or apartment. These are the ones that will bring you back.

√ Keep a stock of various coins and small-denomination bills. Carry only the cash you will need for basic expenses in your pockets. Stow large amounts of cash or traveler's checks in your moneybelt.

√ Use moist towelettes to refresh your face and hands. They help keep your body temperature down. You can find them at convenience stores and pharmacies, often stored in the ice cream freezer.

√ Cool off in a hotel lobby, restaurant, book store or any air conditioned shop. Ice cold fruit juices, soda water, and electrolyte drinks are available in many stores.

√ Always carry copies of the following passport pages.

Title page (with your photo and personal data)
Visa page
Latest entry stamp
Immigration TM card

City Transportation

Bangkok has many types of transportation. The fares are low and there is always a way to get around at any time of day. The network includes overhead trains, motor coaches, city buses, taxis, motorcycle taxis, tuk-tuks, songtaews, and water taxis. It's not unusual to use several of these methods in one day.

Buses

Bangkok's city buses are an effective way to get around. They manage to keep up with the traffic flow in spite of the frequent stops. Take note that these stops are very brief since the passengers don't need to pay the fare as they board.

Each bus has a conductor who collects fares, makes change and gives you a ticket. Keep this handy during the ride since fare inspectors often board the bus and ask to see the passengers' tickets.

Most bus routes are serviced by both air-conditioned and open air buses. The fare is one-price on the open-air buses but on the air-conditioned ones you will need to tell the conductor where you want to go since the fare depends on distance traveled. Tell the conductor the Thai word for a landmark close to your destination such as a temple, department store, bus terminal, train station, school, or major road. Show them the location on the bus map if possible.

Until you get the city wired, knowing when to get off the bus demands all of your attention. If you are seated you can look out the window and follow the progress on the bus map. But if you are standing it's not so easy since you can not see the street signs or landmarks without bending over to look out the windows and there's often not enough room to bend over. If you get lost or pass up your destination, get off the bus and look for a bus going the other way with the same number that you arrived on. If you are on a one way road, the return bus travels on a nearby road.

The buses don't always follow the routes that are shown on the bus map. Construction, high water or other obstructions could cause them to detour. Then comes the question, stay on, or get off? These are the decision points that provide some very interesting excursions in the city.

At stops, buses don't always pull right next to the curb and passengers have to cross one lane of traffic. Be very careful when boarding and getting off of a bus.

Secure a hand hold as soon as you get on the bus since the driver will start off when everyone is on board.

When standing, hold on to the overhead rails or the seat backs and keep your knees bent a little. Sudden stops and starts are the norm and it's easy to lose your balance.

There are pickpockets and bag slashers on the buses so carry your wallet in a front pocket or moneybelt. If you carry a bag, keep it in front of you.

Non Air-Conditioned Buses

These open-window buses are the least expensive way to get around and are identified by their coloring: blue/yellow (the blue bus) and red/yellow (the red bus). The red buses are in better condition than the blue and the fare is higher. The fare is five baht for the blue bus and seven baht for the red bus. The destinations are written in Thai but the bus number is plainly visible on placards in the front windshield and on the side near the rear door. This route number is the one shown on the bus map. If these placards are blue, the bus follows its established route. Red or yellow placards indicate variations such as a shortened route or travel on the expressway.

Air-Conditioned Buses

These are usually less crowded, though standing room only is common during the rush hours. The fares range from 8-16 baht depending on the distance traveled. You will need to tell the conductor where you are going. The number placards are plainly visible in the front windshield and along the side near the rear door.

Micro Buses

Farangs call these "the purple buses". The fare is 25 baht no matter how far you travel. They carry only seated passengers and provide TV, newspapers and magazines.

These buses serve the most popular areas and are an excellent way to investigate the city since the unobstructed view out the windows allows you to see where you are and establish landmarks.

Green Buses

Avoid taking the green buses until you are used to traveling around the city. The fare is only 4 baht but they are reckless with sudden lane changes, swerves, and sudden stops the norm. They are the same size as the micro buses but are not air-conditioned and are usually crowded to standing-room only.

Skytrain

The best addition to the public transport system is the Skytrain

that operates on an elevated platform. It is air-conditioned, roomy and the glare proof windows give you a terrific overview of the city. It is also the fastest way to travel. For example, from Sukhumvit Road to Chatuchak Weekend Market takes less than 10 minutes, by bus the trip takes around 30 minutes. There are currently two lines in operation:

√ The Sukhumvit line that runs from Mo Chit Station on Paholyothin Road (the Chatuchak Weekend Market) to On Nut Station at Sukhumvit Soi 77.

√ The Silom Line that runs between Saphan Taksin Station (Taksin Bridge, Chao Phraya River) and the National Stadium Station on Rama I Road.

The two lines intersect at the Central Station (Siam Square) where there are two platform levels allowing a change of trains. All station platforms are monitored by security cameras and guards. They are accessible by a stairway though some have up-escalators and elevators. There are refreshment kiosks but no toilet facilities at the stations. The trains run from 6 A.M. to midnight and tickets are available only at the stations. Single journey tickets are purchased from a machine that accepts five- and ten-baht coins and the fares range between 10 and 40 baht, depending on the distance traveled. Route maps are available at the stations and other locations.

At the ticket office, multi-trip tickets may be prepaid for 200 baht plus a 30 baht deposit on the ticket. This ticket is returned by the automatic gate as you exit and the cost of each journey is deducted. The remainder of the ticket value is displayed at the exit gate. The ticket may be refilled at the ticket office.

The Skytrain Website
www.2bangkok.com/2bangkok/Skytrain/index.shtml

Taxis

Bangkok has thousands of taxis identified by a rooftop sign, "Taxi Meter," showing the Thai language syntax of adjective after the

noun. There are no taxi ranks so they are always on the move and can be hailed anywhere. Have someone write your destination in Thai, and always carry an assortment of small bills and coins since the drivers may not have change.

Air-conditioned Toyotas are the most common Taxi Meter and are kept in reasonably good condition. Before you get in, tell the driver where you are going so he can decide if he will take you. Some drivers will refuse long distance fares or certain destinations during rush hours. In addition, drivers rent the taxis and must return them at a certain hour, usually at 4 P.M., and they may refuse to take you if your destination is not convenient with their schedule.

Make sure the meter is turned on as soon as the taxi starts off. If the driver says that the meter is broken or pretends not to understand you, tell him to stop, *"yoot."* Then get out and take another taxi. At night, especially in popular areas, many drivers try to negotiate a set price and not use the meter.

Soi Transportation

While metered taxis are always found on the main roads and large sois they rarely cruise the small sois and lanes unless they are dropping off a fare, but the small sois are well served with transportation by *songtaews*, *tuk-tuks*, and motorcycle taxis.

Songtaews

Also called *siilors* or *Subarus*, these small, covered pickup trucks with bench seats in the bed operate on routes that connect the sois with main roads, bus stops, and marketplaces. The fares are around

10 baht. There are no set stops, just flag them down to board and ring the buzzer to get off. They wait for fares at the mouths of busy sois near major roads and markets. You can also hire them to take you to any destination and negotiate the fare.

Tuk-tuks

Every newcomer to Bangkok takes at least one ride on these three-wheeled, open vehicles. They are suitable for short trips in fair weather and are a good way to travel on the sois when looking for an address. The fares are always negotiated beforehand and only marginally cheaper than taxis. The name *tuk-tuk* came from the sound their two-stroke motors make.

Motorcycle Taxis

Despite the reputation of motorcycles as Asia's answer to birth

control, motorcycle taxis may often provide the only transportation to go deep into the sois. The driver should supply you with a helmet but it's really your knees that will concern you the most since the bike weaves in and around traffic at incredibly close distances. Groups of them are found at the mouths of sois, parked along the curb, or can be flagged down on the street. They are identified by brightly colored vests with numbers on the back. The fares depend on the distance and start at 10 baht. You can't get a ride like this at Disneyland.

Boats have been used as taxis since before the founding of the city. Although most of the *klongs* (canals) in Bangkok have been made into streets, there are still several in use, and on the Thonburi side of the river, which is laced with canals, water taxis are a necessity. There, many of the residents who live along the water have personal boats parked beneath the house.

Scheduled ferries cross the river and make several stops along the banks but don't go into the klongs. They are used by school children and workers who regularly travel between Thonburi and Bangkok. The fares depend on how far you are traveling and are collected by a conductor.

Boats that go into the Thonburi klongs are long and narrow with a four cylinder car or truck engine mounted on a pedestal at the rear with a long propeller shaft leading from the engine into the water. It is steered by turning the motor on its pedestal, and when the propeller gets fouled with debris, the driver pushes the steering lever down to raise the prop and clear it. These are called *rua hang yao*, long tailed boats. They roar across the river raising a tall "rooster tail" of water. They are quite fast and give you an exciting ride but you must know where you want to get off and signal the driver when approaching your destination since they do not automatically stop at every landing.

Be especially careful when boarding or disembarking from ferries or water taxis since they don't linger at the landings.

Chao Phraya River Express Ferry

This boat travels the river between the Krung Thep Bridge and Nonthaburi. Fares start at 6 baht depending on the distance travelled. The service runs every 20 minutes between 6 A.M. and 6 P.M. The trip from the landing at the Oriental Hotel to Nonthaburi makes several stops and takes about one hour.

Cross River Ferries

Boats operate between specific landings that are located near major bus lines on both sides of the river. The fare is two baht.

Long-Tail Water Taxis

These craft depart from the Chang Landing near the Grand Palace. They provide service into the klongs on the Thonburi side of the river. Fares from 5 baht.

Saen Saep Ferry

Boats operate on Klong Saen Saep from the Bangkapi intersection in the east to the Pratunam Market, Wat Sakhet, and ends at Banglamphu on the Chao Phraya River. Fare is 5-7 baht.

Notes

Notes

Apartment Hunting

Deciding where in the city to settle down is the biggest question facing a newcomer. Fortunately, the city is practically free of street crime and has no particular area noted for high burglary rates. In addition, any apartment you are likely to rent will provide 24-hour security. Finally, the streets are not all boulevard hustle and throughout the city are many quiet, picturesque sois where you will find a mix of reasonably priced apartment buildings next to high priced condos.

It's usually best to choose the area where you live by what it is you intend to do. If you plan on working, find a place close to where you work or where there is convenient and reliable transportation to various locations. If you are here for health purposes you may wish to live near the hospital. As a rule, if you need easily accessible transportation you will want a place near a major road. If that is not a requirement you can go deeper into the soi, farther from the main roads. There is always transportation available no matter how far in the soi you live. Songtaews drive established routes on various sois, while tuk-tuks and motorcycle taxis cruise around looking for fares. They all go to the mouth of the soi at a major road near a bus stop or can be hired to take you where you wish to go.

Another decision is whether to live in an area where there is a farang community or in one that is completely Thai. I found that living among Thais is a pleasurable experience when, for a couple of years, I rented a two story house deep in a warren of sois in the Lad Prao area.

I was the only farang in the neighborhood and only rarely did I see another Westerner passing through. Next door was a mom & pop store. A few doors away was an old Chinese shop house where a few Thai ladies sat around gossiping while spinning silk in the traditional way. At the end of the soi an assortment of shops and restaurants formed the unofficial community center, especially on Saturdays. Noodle carts, fruit vendors, and even a milkman from a university project cruised the soi ringing bells, honking horns or calling out to announce their presence. *Songtaews* were plentiful in the morning when people were going to work, and in the evening when they returned home. During the day, motorcycle taxis and tuk-tuks cruised the sois.

Every now and then an elephant would stroll down the soi led by its keepers and the Thais would come out of their houses to make an offering by buying bananas to feed the animal. Some would pay a few baht and then walk under the belly of the beast to bring them good luck. It seemed to work, no one was squashed. I call that fortunate.

The neighbors were friendly and helped me to line up a maid, laundry service, home deliveries and other arrangements that were best conducted in Thai language. Once when I had to return to the US for a visit I asked my neighbor, who had lived in New York and spoke English very well, if he could help me line up transportation to the airport with one of the songtaews that came down the soi. Instead, he offered to take me himself in his new Volvo. He didn't mind that it was a morning flight when the traffic would be peaking.

Wherever you choose to live you will have experiences like this. The Thai people make good, though sometimes noisy, neighbors. Even if you are the token farang in a neighborhood you probably won't experience resentment or prejudice unless you are rude or disrespectful.

The city is divided into districts as described below.

Sukhumvit District

This area is bordered by Soi 77 on the east, New Petchburi Rd. on the north, Rama IV Rd. on the south, and Witthayu Rd. (Wireless Rd.) on the west.

Silom District

Adjoins the southwest corner of the Sukhumvit District. It is bordered by Rama IV Rd. on the north, Sathorn Rd. on the southeast, Charoen Krung Rd. on the west, and Si Phraya Rd. to the northwest.

Erawan District

This is bordered by the Sukhumvit District on the east, Rama IV Rd. on the south, Phaya Thai Rd. on the west and Victory Monument on the north.

Dusit District

This area is bordered on the east by Phayathai Rd. and Paholyothin Rd., Si Phraya Rd. on the south, the Chao Phraya River on the west, and Ratchawithi Rd. on the north.

All sections of the city have numerous apartment buildings, department stores, water and gas suppliers, laundries, maids and other living services. If you are looking for employment as a teacher there are dozens of English teaching centers here.

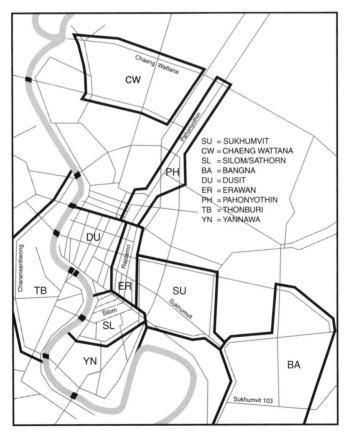

SU = SUKHUMVIT
CW = CHAENG WATTANA
SL = SILOM/SATHORN
BA = BANGNA
DU = DUSIT
ER = ERAWAN
PH = PAHONYOTHIN
TB = THONBURI
YN = YANNAWA

MAP OF GREATER BANGKOK

If you use an apartment-finding service you may be quoted rent prices that can be twice what the locals pay. Never accept their first price. These services will show you photos of what's available.

Rental agreements range from monthly to one-year leases. Deposits are readily returned if you live up to the terms of the contract.

Some apartment buildings have Internet sites describing their facilities. Search for "Bangkok apartments" in your browser. Check out the classified section of the Bangkok Post newspaper where apartments are always advertised, but these are only a few of the vacancies available. Most landlords don't advertise in the Post since it's expensive and the farang market base is small. Instead, they post "For Rent" signs, in English, on utility poles or fences near the apartment building. Some don't even do that so if you see an apartment or condo that you like the looks of, go to the desk and inquire if they have vacancies.

Start by walking the area between Sukhumvit Soi 1 and Soi Asoke. Go into the sois and keep your eyes open for "apartment for rent" signs. Check them all out even if they look pricey, they might not be out of your range and it will give you experience in negotiating with apartment managers. Use your *Robertson's Practical English-Thai Dictionary* and keep a note book, collect business cards and brochures, and above all, take your time. Thais like to do business in a relaxed manner. If the building has a coffee shop, stop in for a break after your tour of the apartment and its facilities.

Next, extend your search to the Sukhumvit Road area between Soi Asoke and Soi Ekamai (Soi 63). Take note that the sois are numbered with the odd numbers on the north side of Sukhumvit and the even numbered sois on the south side. On the city map, this looks like a long distance but it is only about 3 miles. I lived on Soi 61 for a couple of years and occasionally walked from there to Soi 1 in an hour. I did this because, before the Skytrain went into operation, it was often faster than the traffic flow. Now, it's only minutes on the Skytrain. Along this stretch there are apartment buildings and condos in the sois on both sides of the street. Sois 18, 20, 27, 36, 38, 39, 49, 53, 55, 61 and 63 have a number of apartment buildings.

Walking through the area where you're looking for an apartment is the best way to get a feel of the neighborhood. Listen to the noise level. Do you hear dogs barking? The clang of tools from a motorcycle or car repair shop? The roar of trucks or the thump of a pile driver from a nearby construction project? Look for high-water marks on the utility poles and walls bordering the street. Bangkok is at sea level and heavy rain coupled with a high tide can turn some of the sois back into klongs. Are there any mom & pop stores or food shops nearby? Do any taxis, tuk-tuks or motorcycle taxis cruise the area? Is there more than one entrance into the soi? When you find a place you would like to live, revisit the area at different times and on different days, just in case the construction crew was on a break when you first checked it out. Inquire at the front desk of the apartment building about the availability of transportation, shopping, hospital and any other services you require.

All apartments are furnished with bed, settees, chairs, clothes closet, and a table. They have kitchenettes with a sink and refrigerator but in most cases you will need to supply your own cooker. A two-burner, gas stove will suit most of your needs.

There are also town houses for rent. They are advertised in the Bangkok Post and can be found through rental agents. They are often cheaper than apartments but don't provide furniture or maid service. Furniture and appliances can be rented and arrangements can be made for maid service.

Sukhumvit Apartments

The rent for the apartments listed below ranges from $100 -600 a month. They include studio, one-bedroom and two-bedroom apartments. Many are month-to-month rentals, others require lease agreements. All are air-conditioned, fully furnished, and include a kitchenette. Some have a garden area, pool, exercise room, coffee shop, cable TV and Internet hookups.

Street Lodge

Soi 1, Sukhumvit Rd.
Tel 02 254 3572

Studios and one-bedroom apartments from $300 USD per month. Electricity, water, and cable TV are additional. Month to month rental agreement.

Krisda Mansion

11/26 Soi 1, Sukhumvit Rd.
Tel 02 251 8480

One- and two-bedroom apartments from $400 USD per month. Electricity, water, and cable TV are extra. Requires first and last month deposit.

City Mansion

16 Soi 3 (Nana Nua), Sukhumvit Rd.
Tel 02 655 5461   Fax 02 254 4769
www.citymansion.com

One- and two-bedroom apartments from $400 USD per month. Electricity, water charged separately. Monthly rent or six-month lease.

Saranjai Mansion

Soi 6, Sukhumvit Rd.
Tel 02 688 4351

One-bedroom apartments from $350 USD per month. Fully furnished, includes kitchen and living room.

Nantiruj Tower

Soi 8, Sukhumvit Rd.
Tel 02 653 1002   Fax 02 653 1005
na_nantiruj@hotmail.com

Studios, 1 and 2 bedroom apartments from $500 USD per month. Pool, jacuzzi, sauna, exercise room, cable TV.

Chaios Mansion

40 Soi 11, Sukhumvit Rd.
Tel 02 252 5470

One-bedroom apartments from $400 USD per month with six-month lease, includes water and electricity. Has kitchen, maid, laundry. Pool, large garden.

Sooksawasdi Apartment

21/3 Soi 11, Sukhumvit Rd.
Tel 02 651 0153   Fax 02 255 4558

One and two bedroom apartments. Large yard, swimming pool.

Insaf Court

21 Soi 13, Sukhumvit Rd.
Tel 02 255 8273   Fax 02 2455 8274

One bedroom apartment from $350 USD per month. Includes pool and exercise room. Water, electricity and phone are extra.

Star Suites

Soi 15, Sukhumvit Rd.
Tel 02 651 0030

Studio, 1 and 2 bedroom apartments. Pool, sauna, fitness room.

Lin Court

256 Soi 16, Sukhumvit Rd.
Tel 02 208 0354

1 and 2 bedroom apartments. Includes 24-hour security, maid service, telephone, kitchen, pool.

Lakeside Residence

Soi 21 (Asoke) near Sukhumvit Rd.
Tel 02 229 4300
> Fully furnished studios, 1-2 bedroom apartments.

Tarit Court

8 Soi 27, Sukhumvit Rd.
Tel 02 259 0350
taritcourt@yahoo.com
Manager: Khun Oy
> Studio and one bedroom apartments from $100 USD per month. Includes mini-kitchens, phones, security and maid service. Near Sukhumvit Road buses and Skytrain. Very quiet soi.

Serviced Apartments

Most serviced apartments include Internet connections, business centers, laundry, exercise rooms, swimming pools and other amenities.

The rents start at $450 USD and a lease is required.

Euro Park Hotel

27 Soi 1, Sukhumvit Rd.
Tel 02 254 1074   Fax 02 254 1076
europark@a-net.net.th
> Studio, 1 and 2 bedroom serviced apartments with mini-kitchens from $500 USD per month, includes electricity, water, and maid services. Credit cards accepted.

Bright City Tower

21/4 Soi 11, Sukhumvit Rd.
Tel 022 651 0159   Fax 02 254 4567
brightcity@hotmail.com
www.brightcitytower.com
> Studio, 1 and two bedroom apartments from $450 USD. Includes maid, laundry satellite TV, telephone, fax, Internet, microwave, refrigerator.

Grand President

14 Soi 11, Sukhumvit Rd.
Tel 01 651 1200   Fax 02 651 1260

Studio, one and two-bedroom apartments from $500 USD. Includes maid, laundry satellite TV, telephone and other amenities.

Ambassador Palace

18 Soi 11, Sukhumvit Rd.
Tel 02 651 0205   Fax 02 255 7397

Royal President

43 Soi 15 Sukhumvit Rd.
Tel 02 253 9451   Fax 02 253 8959

President Park

95 Soi 24, Sukhumvit Rd.
Tel 02 661 1000   Fax 02 661 1070

Sawadee Villa

58/5-12 Soi 31, Sukhumvit Rd.
Tel 02 651 0205   Fax 02 255 7937

38 Mansion

25/2 Soi 38, Sukhumvit Rd.
Tel 02 381 7603-6   Fax 02 381 7607

The amenities include a business center, direct telephone line, room service, satellite, cable TV, coffee shop, swimming pool, spa pool and sauna.

Apartment Utilities

In most cases, the costs for electricity, telephone, and water are not included in the rent but are charged separately to each apartment.

Electricity

The cost for electricity ranges from three to five baht per unit, but it is common practice for apartment managers to add a surcharge.

Make certain that you understand the electricity rates and amount of surcharge. Some apartments add an additional 40% to the bill. The electric bill is monthly and is determined by the meter inside each apartment. The amount depends a lot on how much you use the air-conditioner.

The current supplied in Bangkok is 240 volts 50 cycles and is not compatible with products made for the American market unless a power adaptor is used. Heavy duty adaptors are available from electric appliance shops for around $10. The wall receptacles are a two-prong (not grounded) type that is peculiar to Thailand.

Power failures are common during the rainy season. When the power is interrupted, throw the master switch to your apartment into the off position to minimize the initial power surge, or unplug the appliances sensitive to power surges such as computers, stereos or VDO systems.

Cooking Gas

Some apartments provide a gas hot water heater and cooking range but you will need to arrange to have bottled LPG gas delivered. A refundable deposit is required on the cylinder that is supplied by the gas shop and delivery is always prompt. The apartment manager can make the arrangements for you but for convenience you should try to learn the drill for ordering gas from the shop over the phone. Keep an extra cylinder on hand and store it outside of the apartment.

Safe stowage and usage is important because this gas is highly flammable. It's the same gas that's used in RVs and boats and you should use the same precautions. Do your cooking in a well ventilated room, porch or balcony. If you suspect a leak, don't try to fix it yourself, call the gas stove shop for repair. Don't use the camp style cooker that attaches directly to the gas bottle. They are unsafe.

Telephone Services and Costs

The charges that tenants pay for telephone use will vary according to the rental agreement. In any case, they are likely to be very low, unless you make numerous overseas calls.

Check the cost of a local call. Most apartments charge a rate of 5 baht for 15 minutes of usage. For individually owned apartments or houses, the charge is usually the telephone company's charge of

3 baht per call but you may be required to pay an additional monthly fee of 100 baht.

Find out how many lines are connected to the switchboard and the number of apartments.

Check to see if the switchboard is automatic and if calls can be made to your room directly.

Check the congestion level of the switchboard by calling the apartment for inquiries at different times of the day.

Some apartments disconnect the phone line after 15 minutes of use, others after only 5 minutes of use. This may be a problem if you intend to use the lines for Internet connections.

Check the cost of making an international call and if you can make these calls directly from your room.

Laundry

The apartment buildings have staff on hand to do laundry, but they may refuse to wash underwear. Alternatively, you could take your clothes to a laundry and dry cleaning shop. Ask the apartment manager for the location.

Water Supply

Apartments are billed monthly for city water services. Make sure you know the rate before you move in. It's customary for the management to add a surcharge to the water bill. Some apartments charge less than others.

Use tap water only for bathing, laundry and dishes. It is not pure enough to drink without being filtered at the taps. Various filters are available at a reasonable price.

Use only purified water for drinking and cooking. There are several water companies that deliver to your door at no extra charge.

Apartment managers often keep a stock of bottled water on hand or will arrange to have deliveries made to your apartment. Bottled water comes in different sizes: one liter bottles, 5 liter bottles and 5 gallon jugs.

The 5 gallon size is very economical and a stand-up water cooler can be rented that dispenses hot as well as cold water. I used this water for years and never had a problem with the purity.

Boon Rawd (Singha Water)
Tel 02 241 1361

M Water Co. (Sprinkle Water)
Tel 02 998 1350

Mountain Spring
Tel 02 913 2251

Siam Drinking Water
Tel 02 322 8565

Notes

Shopping

Bangkok is an international city that offers products from all over the world, and if you can't find what you need you can have it made. It's truly the land of free enterprise with marketing venues ranging from street vendors to fashionable department stores, often selling the exact same items, though the street price is much lower.

Department stores and supermarkets are fairly evenly priced and those favored by expats usually have some English speaking staff.

Cash is the preferred method of payment, though international credit cards are acceptable at some department stores and shops. Department store chains provide in-store credit cards to approved customers.

Bargaining is acceptable at tourist shops, street stalls and open markets, but negotiate respectfully, not as a contest of wills. Department stores don't bargain but if you are buying an expensive item and paying in cash, ask for a discount and quite often this is easily granted. No bargaining with restaurants, pharmacies or food purchases.

One curious form of marketing is that shops selling the same kinds of merchandise often group themselves in one area. This is true of many upscale shopping centers like Pantip Plaza as well as the open air areas such as Chinatown and Chatuchak markets.

A good shopping guide is *Nancy Chandler's Map of Bangkok*, available in bookstores.

Shopping Centers

These air conditioned shopping malls are anchored around a department store chain, such as Robinsons, Central, and Isetan. The shops include clothing, shoes, jewelry, books, toys, electronics, appliances, and furniture, both locally produced and imported. They also contain several restaurants, movie theaters, skating rinks, video game parlors and areas for special promotions. They are located in most areas of the city and are open from 10 or 11 A.M. until 9 or 10 P.M.

Mah Boon Krong Center (MBK)

Located at the corner of Rama I Rd. and Phaya Thai Rd., opposite Siam Square.

This center is popular with locals for general merchandise with fair, sometimes negotiated, prices. It includes shops for clothing, leather goods, shoes, electronics, jewelry, music, furniture, and restaurants. Tokyu Department store is the anchor.

Amarin Plaza

Located on Ploenchit Rd., near the Erawan Shrine.

Sogo Department Store is the anchor and the shops sell mainly shoes, jewelry, and ladies' apparel.

Emporium

Located at 622 Sukhumvit Rd. at Soi 24. www.emporiumThailand.com.

Here are numerous specialty stores featuring designer labels. The mall includes a coffee shop, restaurants, music store, portrait studio, supermarket, and movie theaters.

World Trade Center

Located at Rama I Rd. and Rajadamri Rd.

A modern and very large center with Isetan and Zen Central department stores. Dozens of small shops for books, fabrics, furniture, homewares, clothing, and more. Entertainment facilities include an ice skating rink, movie theaters, restaurants. It takes a few hours to go through the center.

Pantip Plaza

Located on Petchburi Rd. west of Rajadamri Rd.
A five story, computer superstore with everything from software to mainframes.

Department Stores

All shopping centers have a well-known department store as an anchor. Here are the two, most well known chains. They are so prominent in Bangkok that they are often used as landmarks when giving directions.

Central Department Stores

Chidlom, 1027 Ploenchit Rd.
Lad Prao, 1691 Paholyothin Rd.
Silom, 306 Silom Rd.
Silom Complex, 191 Silom Rd.
A major department store with branches in many locations. Hours from 10 A.M. to 9 P.M.

Robinson's Department Stores

Silom Store, 2 Silom Rd.
Sukhumvit Store, 259 Sukhumvit Rd. at Soi 19
Well stocked supermarkets with a wide range of general merchandise. Hours from 10:30 A.M. to 9 P.M.

Open Air Markets

Open air shopping is a way of life for Bangkokians. Street vendors and markets are everywhere in the city selling meat, seafood, vegetables, fruit, clothing, shoes, household goods, ceramics, crafts, luggage, pets, and items too numerous to list. In addition, except for food items, bargaining is not only permitted it's expected. In many cases, the quality of goods sold by street or stall vendors is the same as that from department stores.

Chinatown

Although not a "marketplace" in the strict sense of the word, it is the largest section of the city that is devoted to commerce. Established by Chinese traders more than 200 years ago it is still a thriving hub of activity where practically everything imaginable is sold. Even if you are not looking to buy something it is an unique experience just to explore the area.

Many of the buildings are more than 80 years old, crammed together so close in places that the lanes between them are only wide enough for motorcycles to pass through. Although it may appear confusing and even risky to walk around the area, I have been there many times, day and night, and have never been accosted or had a problem with theft. At night, after the stores have closed, street vendors set up shop on some of the sois selling everything from pirated copies of the latest movies to snake-blood cocktails made from a freshly killed cobra and Mekong whiskey. The preparation is a sight you won't soon forget.

Chinatown is not confined within definable borders but its center is Yaowarat Road between Songsawat Road on the east and Chakwarat Road on the west. You can get there from Sukhumvit Road on the air-conditioned bus number 1, non air-conditioned busses 25 or 40, or micro busses numbers 5, 14, or 34. These will take you into Chinatown on Yaowarat Road and make their return on Charoen Krung Road, the road north of Yaowarat. A good way to tour Chinatown is with *Nancy Chandler's Map of Bangkok*, which contains detailed descriptions of the area's layout.

Areas of Interest in Chinatown

Yaowarat Road
This street has numerous shops selling 24 karat gold jewelry at the current world price which is posted daily in front of the shop. Each of these mirror-lined shops employs a Sikh guard who sits near the door wearing a turban and cradling a shotgun. Also on the road are restaurants featuring bird's nest and shark's fin soups, herbal medicine shops, opera theaters, department stores and street vendors.

Ban Mo
This area along Pharuhat Road is the lair of silversmiths and jewelry supply shops. You will know when you are near there by the tapping of the smiths' hammers resounding from the shops.

Nakhon Kasem Market
Also known as the Thieves Market, this nest of pawnshops is sited in the maze of alleys bordered by Charoen Krung Road, Yaowarat Road, Chakrawat Road and Boriphut Road.

Pahurat Cloth Market
Also called the Indian Market, this area is located at the western end of Sampeng Lane across Chakraphet Road. Entrance to this market is through the shops that line the street. Here are batik and print sarongs as well as fabrics for clothing, curtains and bedding from all over Asia.

Sampeng Lane
This narrow lane sells a wide range of products but many of them are sold only in wholesale lots. It is packed with shoppers and takes an hour to go from the eastern end of the lane at Songsawat Road to the western end at Chakraphet Road.

Chatuchak Weekend Market

Located at the intersection of Paholyothin Rd. and Kamphaengphet Rd. At the Mo Chit station of the Skytrain Sukhumvit line.

Open Saturday and Sunday from 8 A.M. to 5 P.M. There are more than 9000 stalls in this market. Price bargaining is expected. *Nancy Chandler's Map of Bangkok* includes a layout of the market.

Klongtoey

Located at the corner of Rama IV Rd. and Ratchada Rd.
This market is located near the Sukhumvit area. It sells fruit, vegetables, meat and seafood as well as wearing apparel.

Lang Krasuang

Located at the intersection of Ratchadamnoen Klang Rd. and Atsadang Rd., near the Royal Hotel.
This area runs along Atsadang Road and specializes in used goods, cameras, musical instruments, electronics and assorted items.

Pratunam

Located at the corner of Ratchaprarop Rd. and Petchburi Rd., next to the Indra Hotel.
This market specializes in clothing fabrics and accessories for tailors and also sells ready made clothing either singly or in wholesale lots.

Supermarkets

There are many supermarkets in the city that stock imported food items as well as locally made products. These markets are accustomed to dealing with farangs and most have English speaking staff on hand. You can also arrange to have your purchases delivered to your home and some stores will even take telephone orders. Most department stores and shopping centers have markets with a wide selection of western foods.

Emporium

Sukhumvit Rd. at the corner of Soi 24
This shopping center has a supermarket on the 5th floor.

Foodland

Soi Patpong 1, Silom Rd.
Sukhumvit Soi 5
"The Land of Food" as its motto states has a full range of products and very helpful staff. Open 24 hours.

Tops Marketplace

Central Chidlom, Ploenchit Rd.
Miracle Mall, Sukhumvit Rd. at Soi 41
Robinsons, Sukhumvit Rd. at Soi 19
www.tops.co.th.

This store has English-speaking staff as well as signs in English. It has a delicatessen, bakery, meat counter, and a complete range of grocery and non-food items. Some stores open 24 hours. Home delivery available.

Villa Supermarkets

Sukhumvit Rd. at the corner of Soi 33
Ploenchit Center, Sukhumvit Soi 2

In business more than 20 years, this store stocks imported and specialty, food items. The store at Sukhumvit Soi 33 is an unofficial meeting place for the expat community and has a bulletin board for the expatriate community to use.

Bakeries

Bangkok provides a wide range of excellent French, Danish, German, and American bakeries. Some of the best are located in the major hotels such as The Oriental, The Regent, the Le Meridien, The President, The Landmark, and the Grand Hyatt Erawan. All the supermarkets have a bakery section or a bakery nearby. There are also dozens of small bakeries, often combined with delicatessens or restaurants.

Au Bon Pain

Sindhorn Bldg., 2nd Flr., Wireless Rd.
Lake Rajada Office Complex, Sukhumvit Soi 16
Ploenchit Center, 1st Flr., Sukhumvit Soi 2

These bakeries have breads, pastries, muffins, cookies, bagels as well as soups and sandwiches. They provide on-site cafe, take away, or delivery.

Bei Otto

1 Sukhumvit Soi 20

A German restaurant and bakery with a large assortment of bread, rolls, pastries and cakes.

Cheesecake House

69/2 Sub-soi 20 (Shamchan) Sukhumvit Soi 55

This bakery maintains a complete selection of cheesecakes, pies, cakes, and cookies. Home delivery is provided.

Danish Bakery

Sukhumvit Soi 33/1, next to Villa Market.

Danish breads, pastries and cakes.

La Boulange Bakery

On Convent Rd. near Silom Rd.

A French bakery with a large assortment of breads, pastries and cakes -- has a cafe on site.

Deli and Imported Food

Supermarkets carry a wide range of delicatessen items as well as shops that specialize in these foods.

Be Lucky

Soi Wat Prok 1, Soi St. Louis 3, Sathorn Tai Rd.

German sausages, delicatessen meats and cheeses.

Cutting Edge

Soi Ruam Rudi (opposite Holy Redeemer Church)

Carries a wide range of imported delicatessen items.

Bei Otto

1 Sukhumvit Soi 20

A German delicatessen with a wide variety of freshly packed sausage and cheeses.

Notes

94

Banking, Credit Cards

Thai banks are efficient and provide the customary personal and business accounts, as well as ATM, telephone, and computer banking services.

It's a good idea to open an account with either Bangkok Bank or Thai Farmers Bank. It needn't be large, just enough to keep the account open. These banks are not only recognized internationally but also have connections with American banks. This association makes the transfer of funds much simpler and less expensive.

Banks

Major Thai banks have branches throughout the kingdom and provide currency exchange kiosks in tourist areas. Banks are open from 8:30 A.M. to 3:30 P.M., Monday to Friday, except holidays. Currency exchange kiosks have varied office hours, many are open 8:30 A.M. to 10:00 P.M. every day. The authorized money exchange counters at hotels are open 24 hours a day.

Communication in main branches is seldom a problem since clerks usually speak at least some English and many bank forms are written in English as well as Thai.

You can open a savings account in a Thai bank by presenting your passport with a valid visa. A savings account can be opened with a minimum deposit of 100 baht. After an account has been approved, you can get a Bualuang ATM card that can be used at over 1,000 ATMs located throughout the country. Upon further approval, a Bualuang Premier ATM card can be obtained. This card extends the service of Bualuang ATM to include the withdrawal of cash abroad using any overseas ATM within the PLUS system that includes over 200,000 machines worldwide.

Checks drawn on Thai banks and made to you can be deposited in your savings account without any problem. They are generally cleared within a day but checks drawn on foreign banks can take several weeks to clear.

You can also open a checking account but you must show proof of residency, a rent receipt in your name is the usual document. Most expats don't use a checking account and a lot of Thais don't either, preferring instead to pay wages and make purchases in cash. A friend of mine once sold his house to a Thai-Chinese woman who paid him 2 million baht, in cash. "She showed up riding a bicycle, carrying a Central Department Store shopping bag full of Thai currency," he told me. In the US, this woman would have been suspected as a bank robber or drug dealer but in Thailand it's business as usual.

Bank Deposits

Don't make large deposits of American dollars into a Thai bank until you understand the rules and policies for withdrawals. All banks are not equal and government banking regulations are subject to change.

Cash bonds, in baht, are required for resident or retirement visas but although this deposit is refundable when the visa is cancelled, the funds are subject to the fluctuations in value while they are held in Thailand. For example, a retiree who posted a bond in 1996 when 25 baht equalled $1, could only watch as the Asian economy crashed in 1997 to the point where nearly 50 baht were required to buy one dollar.

Thai Banks

Listed below are the head offices of prominent Thai banks where you can open accounts. In order to make cash withdrawals from a branch office you need to file a signature verification card with the branch. You will need to show your passport to withdraw funds from a branch other than the ones where your signature card is filed.

Bangkok Bank

333 Silom Rd.
Tel 02 231 4333   **Fax 02 231 4233**
www.bbl.co.th

Siam Commercial Bank

9 Ratchadapisek Rd., Lad Yao
Tel 02 544 2828   **Fax 02 937 7645**
www.scb.co.th

Thai Farmers Bank

1 Soi Thai Farmers Lane, Rat Burana Rd.
Tel 02 470 1199   **Fax 02 470 1144**

U.S. Banks

Bank of America

2/2 Wireless Rd., Bank of America Center
Tel 02 251 6333   Fax 02 254 4003

Chase Manhattan Bank

20 Sathorn Nua (North) Rd., Bubhajit Bldg.
Tel 02 234 5992   Fax 02 234 8386

Citibank

82 Sathorn Nua (North) Rd.
Tel 02 232 2000   Fax 02 639 2560

ATM Banking

Automatic teller machines are located at banks as well as some shopping centers but a service charge will be made on interbank withdrawals. Errors do occur so check your receipt each time you use the ATM.

The withdrawal limits from ATM machines vary from bank to bank, depending on your daily card limit. Thai Farmers Bank has a maximum of 50,000 baht per day. The average cost is 60 to 65 baht per transaction.

Some machines run-out of cash, especially on Sunday nights, or occasionally malfunction and keep your card. You may wish to maintain two bank accounts, in the same or a different bank, and carry two ATM cards.

If you have an account with the Bank of America you can use the ATM at various banks in Bangkok.

Credit Cards

Credit cards are widely accepted throughout the kingdom. One safeguard for lost or stolen cards is Credit Card Sentinel www.creditcardsentinel.com.au

American Express

388 Pahonyothin Rd., SP Bldg.
Tel 02 273 5100   After hours Tel 02 273 0022
Hours   Monday to Friday 8 A.M. to 5 P.M.

Diners Club

191 Silom Rd., 12th Fl. Silom Bldg.
Tel 02 238 2920   After hours Tel 02 238 2680

Master Card

Tel 02 256 7326 (24 hours) for lost or stolen cards.

Visa

Tel 02 256 7326 (24 hours) for lost or stolen cards.

Traveler's Checks

Hotels, tourist shops, retailers, and travel agents will cash traveler's checks but their rate of exchange is lower than the bank's. The official rate of exchange is displayed at banks and currency exchanges. You will need to show your passport when cashing traveler's checks.

American Express

Suite 88-92, 8th Floor, Phaya Thai Plaza
128 Phaya Thai Rd., Rajathivi, 10400
Tel 02 216 5183   02 216 5934

Money Transfers

A simple way to receive funds from the US is to open a bank account with the Bank of America (B of A), or an affiliated bank in the US and use the ATM card in Bangkok. For larger amounts, have the funds sent electronically through the SWIFT system to the head office, not a branch, of the Thai bank where you maintain an account.

Money remitted through SWIFT is paid in cash or credited to your savings account, in baht. Remittances can also be directed to commercial dollar accounts where they are credited in US dollars.

Whenever money is sent between countries, both the sending and receiving banks apply transfer charges. But these costs are higher when the US bank has no direct correspondent bank in Thailand. For this reason, it is best to maintain an account with a US bank that is affiliated with a Thai bank.

SWIFT Money Transfer

Society of Worldwide Interbank Financial Telecom is commonly used by Thai banks. There are three designations for sending funds from the US to Thailand through the SWIFT method of transfer.

BEN -- The beneficiary pays for all the costs of the transaction. They are deducted from the amount of the funds sent.

SHA -- The sender and receiver share the costs. The sender pays the costs for sending and the recipient's bank deducts the fees from the amount being sent.

OUR -- The sender pays all the costs involved and the recipient gets the "net amount" of the funds sent.

Thai banks routinely process the SWIFT money transfer within two days and the funds are collectible on the third day after being received by the bank.

Western Union

Money may also be sent through Western Union. Check out the Website, **www.westernunion.com** for details. To collect the money the recipient must show his passport or ID card and the account number Western Union has provided the sender who has forwarded it to the recipient.

Foreign Exchange Control

Foreign visitors may freely bring in foreign bank notes or other types of foreign money. Upon leaving Thailand, a visitor may take out the equivalent of the funds he brought into Thailand. However, this amount is limited to 10,000 US dollars unless the visitor has declared a higher amount upon arrival. Though not legally required, forms to declare the amount of foreign currency you are arriving with are available at the Immigration Department counters where you enter the country.

Changes on the requirement to declare funds brought into Thailand are currently under review. Check the Thai Consulate website for the latest regulations.

Attempts to take out of the country amounts higher than 10,000 USD without having the proper arrival declaration can lead to arrest, confiscation of the excess funds, and prosecution.

According to the brochure, "Exchange Regulations in Thailand", published by the Foreign Exchange Department of the Bank of Thailand, there is "no restriction on the amount of Thai currency that may be brought into the country. A person travelling to Thailand's bordering countries and to other countries may take out local currency up to baht 100,000 and baht 50,000 respectively without authorization. Foreign tourists are freely allowed to take out gold ornaments."

Personal Taxation

For tax purposes, foreigners in Thailand are classified as "residents" or "non-residents." A resident is a person who resides in the kingdom for 180 days in one calendar year, and this duration is cumulative. If you make several visits to Thailand between January and December that add up to 180 days you need a tax clearance before you are allowed out of the country.

Any foreigner, whether a resident or a non-resident, who earns money while living in Thailand must pay tax on income gained from business, salaries, or commissions.

A non-resident is taxed only on income from sources in Thailand.

A resident of Thailand is liable for taxes on income from sources in Thailand as well as on the portion of income from foreign sources that is brought into Thailand.

Consult with a tax consultant for the ever changing details of this requirement.

JPB Business Services

Times Square Bldg., Suite 211
Sukhumvit Rd., between Sois 12 and 14
Open from 10 A.M. to 10 P.M.

Provides Internet service, international phone calls, printing, scanning, photocopying as well as assistance on work permits, visas, business setup, income taxes, and translation services.

Notes

Notes

Communications, Media

Thailand's fast track economic growth in the 1980s and early 1990s spurred the communications sector into the modern age with efficient mail services, satellite phone connections, Internet connections and cable TV stations.

Mail

The postal service has no problem delivering letters with the addresses printed in English using capitalized, block letters. When you send mail or packages, clearly print the sender and receiver addresses in block letters.

You will be notified when parcels from overseas are received and you will need to claim them at the Post Office or the Customs Office. You may be required to pay import duty on these items.

When you send parcels, do not wrap them until the contents have been inspected at the Post Office. There is a parcel wrapping service at each post office that wraps and seals the package for a nominal cost. Parcel post shipping to the US can be done by sea-mail (2 to 3 months delivery time) or by air mail (10-12 days).

If you wish, you can have mail addressed to you C/O GPO BANGKOK, THAILAND with the words POSTE RESTANTE and receive it at the General Post Office on Charoen Krung Road.

Post Offices

Post and Telegraph Office (Main GPO)

Charoen Krung Rd. near the Surawong Rd. intersection. Open 24 hours.

Sukhumvit Area

Soi 23 Sukhumvit, 1/2 block north of Sukhumvit Rd.
Sukhumvit Rd. between Soi 36 and 38
Sukhumvit Rd. near the corner of Soi 4 (Nana)
Sukhumvit Rd., on 2nd floor of the Bangkok Bank across from the Ambassador Hotel.

Shipping Services

Bangkok is a city founded on international trade and a large, well organized shipping industry is firmly established. There are hundreds of agencies experienced in shipping any quantity of commercial goods as well as household items. They are listed in the phone book.

The international express companies are also present in the kingdom and offer guaranteed delivery times and shipment tracking services.

Express Delivery Companies

DHL Worldwide Express

22nd Fl., Grand Amarin Tower
1550 New Petchburi Rd.
Tel: 207-0600 (for customer service)
www.dhl.com/main_index.html

FedEx

8th Fl., Green Tower
3656/22-23 Rama IV Rd.
Tel: 367-3222 (for customer service)
www.fedex.com

Telephone Communications

Emergency Numbers

Police	191
Crime	195
Fire	199
Tourist Police	1155
Highway Police	1153
Ambulance/Rescue	1554
Medical Emergency	1669
Missing Persons	02 282 1815

Calls Within Bangkok

Except for the above listing, all Bangkok telephone numbers must be preceded by 02. For example: 02 xxx xxxx.

International Calls

Placing international calls through hotel phones is the most expensive, but usually the most effective.

Internet Cafes provide the cheapest overseas calls, but the downside is that they are routed via the Internet causing communications breakup, static and lag.

IDT phone cards must have the local Thai access number. Many of those sold in the US do not have this number but it can be requested. Make certain it works before you leave the US by dialing **011-66-access number.**

Long distance rates vary according to the time of day.

Peak Hours	7 A.M. to 9 P.M.
Off-peak Hours	5 A.M. to 7 A.M. and 9 P.M. to 12 A.M.
Budget Hours	12 A.M. to 5 A.M.

Domestic Calls

Domestic calls include not only Thailand, but also Malaysia and Laos. To call anywhere in the kingdom use the STD dialing and refer to the area codes listed in the phone book.

Dial 101 if you want the operator to connect you for a domestic call.

The lowest rates are between 10 P.M. and 7 A.M.

Information Operator

Most operators speak English and will provide any number changes and addresses as required.

Bangkok Metropolitan Area	**Dial 13**
For numbers in the provinces	**Dial 183**

Telephone Directories

The Bangkok Metropolitan Area phone directory is printed in Thai and English versions. Note that Thais are listed by their first name and foreigners are listed by their last name.

The residential phone book is separate from the commercial one (Yellow Pages). The business centers located in hotels have a complete set of phone books and they can also be found at the US Chamber of Commerce library located near the US Embassy on Wireless Road. The Chamber of Commerce also has phone books of major American cities.

Directories can be obtained from:

Shinawatra Directories Co. Ltd.

25th Fl., Shinawatra Tower
500 Paholyothin Rd.
Tel: 02 299-5000

Teleinfo Media Co. Ltd.

1376/1 Nakhon Chaisri Rd.
Bangkok 10300
Tel 02243 8998 Fax 02 243 9010
customerservice@teleinfomedia.net
www.teleinfomedia.net

Internet Communications

Cyber Cafes

Cyber Cafe

Ploenchit Centre, Sukhumvit Rd.
cybercafe@chomanan.co.th
Open 10 A.M. to 10 P.M.
> This cafe has 21 computers and serves refreshments.

JPB Business Services

Times Square Bldg., Suite 211
Sukhumvit Rd. between Sois 12 and 14
Open from 10 A.M. to 10 P.M.
> Provides Internet service, international phone calls, printing, scanning, photocopying as well as assistance on work permits, visas, business setup, income taxes, and translation services.

Cyber Restaurant

Ambassador Hotel, Sukhumvit 13
amplaza@infonews.co.th
Open 24 hours a day
> A full range of food and beverages is served.
> 30 computers, a color printer and scanner.

Internet Service Providers

Loxley Information Services - www.loxinfo.co.th

Internet Thailand - www.inet.co.th

Samart Cybernet - www.samart.co.th/index.php

Newspapers, Magazines

Many newsstands and book stores stock English language magazines, both in Thailand and imported publications.

Local English Language Newspapers

Two English language, daily newspapers are printed in Bangkok, the *Bangkok Post* and *The Nation*. Both cover local, regional and international events and advertise jobs and accommodations for foreigners in the classified section. The Friday editions include a section called "Real Time" in the Post and "Weekend" in the Nation that list weekend social events, movies, concerts, and performances. The papers are available at hotels, newsstands, or home delivery.

Bangkok Post

Tel: 240 3700

The Nation

Tel: 317 1400

International English Language Newspapers

Foreign publications are available at newsstands , hotels, book shops, large department stores and supermarkets. Listed here are just a few.

Wall Street Journal

International Herald Tribune

Daily Telegraph

San Francisco Chronicle

New York Herald Tribune

Local English Language Magazines

Metro Magazine
Thailand Indochina Traveller
Sawadii
Living in Thailand

International Magazines

The Economist
Time Magazine
Newsweek
Far Eastern Economic Review

Radio and TV Stations

There are over 75 radio stations in the Bangkok Metropolitan area and several of them broadcast in English. The music selections include classical, jazz, and rock as well as Thai music.

Local Radio Stations

The following are English speaking stations.
95.5 FM Gold FMX
105 FM Smooth
105.5 FM Easy

Overseas Radio Stations

Shortwave broadcasts from overseas are presented on a regular schedule. Check the *Bangkok Post* Friday insert, "Real Time" for details.
British Broadcasting World Service (BBC)
Voice of America (VOA)
ABC Radio Australia

Television Stations

There are three commercial channels that broadcast in Thai language. There are also several Megaliths language cable channels including CNN, BBC, UBC as well as German, French, and Japanese language channels.

Many apartment buildings provide cable television service with the lease.

Notes

Notes

Bumrungrad Hospital Foyer

Health Care

Personal health is the anxiety shared by all newcomers to Thailand and this concern is not baseless since the tropics are host to bacteria and diseases that are unknown in temperate climates. But you can avoid, or at least minimize the effects of, most health hazards if you follow a set of preventive guidelines and early treatment.

The improvement of public health care has always been a priority of the monarchy who have founded and funded many institutions for the research and treatment of diseases that are prevalent in the country. Laboratories are well equipped to diagnose an illness and doctors follow established procedures for treatment. What's more, medical services are available to all people regardless of economic or social status.

It takes some newcomers a couple of months to become acclimatized to tropical weather and keeping your body cool is the primary goal. The warm temperature requires a greater intake of fluids to counter dehydration and the humidity can cause you to tire faster than in your home country. Don't try to do too much in one day. When possible, plan your day's must-do activities for the morning or early evening hours when it's the coolest. Don't feel guilty about taking a nap and a refreshing shower in the heat of the day.

Food, Water

Anytime American expats meet they mention the food and its effects on their digestive system. It's an American thing, and while you can certainly get Bangkok Belly from bacteria in the food or water you can also get sick from a meal at a fast food restaurant in Seattle. For openers, don't eat raw seafood or meat, which is not difficult since there are only a few Thai meals that are not thoroughly cooked at a high heat. Whether you eat at a street stall or walk-in restaurant choose one that has a lot of customers and use your judgement as to the hygienic conditions of the place.

But even the cleanliness of a restaurant is no guarantee since a sparkling clean American fast food restaurant in Bangkok was guilty of storing its pre-made sandwiches too long causing the mayonnaise to go off and afflicting several customers with a painful bout of diarrhea. This condition can be treated at a clinic or with medication from a pharmacy.

Water

Purified, bottled water is available at convenience stores, markets and everywhere beverages are sold. When you order water in a restaurant a bottle will be brought to your table and opened there or you will be served a glass of *nam chaa*, a weak tea that has been boiled to purify it. Never drink tap water that has not been boiled for at least 20 minutes, filtering alone will not purify the water of bacteria. The quality of ice used in drinks is usually very good, but if it looks dirty, don't use it.

Immunization

The necessity and effectiveness of immunization shots can vary. To find out more check with hospitals and the Travel Medicine and Vaccination Center (TMVC) Tel: 02 655 1024.

AIDS

There is a high incidence of AIDS in Thailand and since no vaccine is available the only preventive action is caution. It is transmitted through sexual contact, contaminated blood used in transfusion, and the use of contaminated needles.

Cholera

Immunization is no longer recommended because of its limited duration of protection. The best protection is to carefully select the food and drink you consume.

Hepatitis A

Usually contracted through contaminated food or water, especially under-cooked meat and seafood. Symptoms include jaundiced eyes and skin, as well as extreme tiredness.

Hepatitis B

This is transmitted through blood, saliva and other body fluids. The highest transmission is through sexual contact.

Rabies

This disease is prevalent in all of Asia and is very serious. Though routinely associated with dogs, the virus can be carried in the salivary glands of any warm-blooded animal, cats, monkeys, or rodents. Be very cautious around any animal that appears sick since the symptoms of the disease can vary. If you have a pet it must be inoculated by a qualified veterinarian. If you are bitten by any animal, even your own pet, wash the wound thoroughly with soap and water, then apply alcohol and go to your doctor or to the Rabies Unit of the Thai Red Cross Society in Bangkok, Tel: 02 252 016 Ext. 27.

Tetanus

If you have never been immunized the full course of shots is recommended. You will need a booster shot every ten years to keep the protection current.

Tuberculosis

This disease is prevalent in all of Southeast Asia. See a doctor if you develop a persistent cough or other symptoms of the malady.

Typhoid

The best protection is personal and household hygiene although an oral vaccine is available.

Dengue Fever

While Bangkok is free from malaria, it does have the Aedes mosquito that carries dengue fever. Symptoms include severe headache and bone ache, a skin rash and fever and chills. There is no immunization for this disease so measures must be taken around your house to prevent the breeding of mosquitoes. Remove puddles of standing water, change water in flower vases daily, and keep water drains clear.

Medical Care

One of the least known facts about Bangkok is the high quality medical care that is available at very low costs. Europeans and Japanese have been coming here for decades for heart surgery, eye surgery, skin surgery, cosmetic surgery and other medical procedures.

During our time in Thailand my wife and I had a few occasions when we had to go to the hospital for minor injuries. Once, she was involved in a tuk-tuk accident and split her scalp about an inch or so. She took a taxi to Samitivej Hospital where a doctor showed up within 5 minutes and treated the wound. The cost was $35 US including the prescription medicine.

My wife was immediately attended to without any preliminary paperwork and for minor emergencies this is often the case. But for major operations the hospitals require a deposit up to 20,000 baht (about $500) and maybe your passport, or proof of medical insurance, before admission. The hospital bill must be settled before you are released and most will accept major credit cards or personal checks drawn on a Thai bank.

Diagnosis, treatment and medication of other ailments are just as reasonably priced. Single occupancy hospital rooms with three meals, TV, air conditioning, and daily delivery of the Bangkok Post newspaper costs less than $50 USD a day.

The medical system is based on the US model. The doctors and surgeons are accredited and many have worked in Europe or the US for several years and speak English. Except in emergencies, the patient and doctor relationship is like a partnership between two adults discussing problems and options. I have never had a Thai doctor or dentist talk down to me or try to sell me more than I needed.

Nurses are well trained, efficient, courteous, and very caring. I have found these characteristics to be consistent in all levels of hospitals, from the lowest priced to the most expensive.

An American friend was involved in a motorcycle accident and broke his leg, shoulder and dented some other parts. He was short on money at the time and could only afford to go to the Police Hospital near the Chao Phraya River. I was skeptical about the care he might receive there for $2 a day, including meals, and visited him often over the months he spent on his back with his encased leg and arm suspended above him by wires. He came out very well. The doctor's fees and medication were very reasonable. The care he received was attentive, and he emerged without infection or other after effects. He still lives in Thailand, travelling around the country for a beneficial organization that gives prosthetic limbs to amputees. That's a curious twist of karma.

I recently went to Bumrungrad Hospital where I had a cataract removed and a permanent lens inserted into my left eye. I had three visits with the doctor for pre- and post-operation exams and a surgery session that lasted about 2 hours. The vision has been improved remarkably and there were no problems. The entire bill came to $870.

Some hospitals accept US insurance payments. Check with your insurance agent to determine if your coverage extends overseas. Blue Cross medical insurance is available in Thailand and since the medical costs are so reasonable, so are the insurance premiums. An American friend of mine, his wife and two kids are insured for 3600 baht ($85 USD) per year. His kids were recently treated for dengue fever (at the same time) and the hospital bill came to 18,000 baht ($420) of which 14,000 baht ($325 USD) was paid by Blue Cross insurance.

Here is a list of Bangkok's hospitals that are favored by the expatriate community. They are staffed by specialists in internal medicine, cardiology, breast cancer, neurology, immunology, gastroenterology, dermatology, cosmetic surgery, dentistry, and eyes, ears, nose and throat treatments. Many of the doctors and surgeons have trained in Europe and the US and speak English as well as other languages.

Hospitals

Bangkok Adventist Mission Hospital

430 Phitsanulok Rd.
Tel 02 281 1422   Fax 02 280 0441
Located near Khao San Road in the Bang Lum Phu area. English
is spoken.

Bangkok Christian Hospital

124 Silom Rd.
Tel 02 634 0560   Fax 02 236 2911
English is spoken.

Bangkok General Hospital

2 Soi 7, Soi Soonvijai, New Petchburi Rd.
Tel 02 318 0066   Fax 02 310 3367
admin@bgh.co.th
www.bgh.co.th
Specialists in ears, nose and throat Helicopter ambulance service.
English spoken.

BNH Hospital (Bangkok Nursing Home)

9/1 Convent Rd. Silom Nua
Tel 02 632 0552   Fax 02 632 0577-9
ENT Center Tel 02 632 0550
Acupuncture/ traditional medicine Tel 02 632 0560
info@bangkoknursinghome.com
www.bangkoknursinghome.com
Established more than 100 years, this hospital is held in high esteem
by both expats and Thais. The staff includes overseas trained
specialists in every field of medicine who are fluent in English,
French, and German. Expat services include overseas insurance
connections. Full range of the latest medical equipment and
facilities. Out-patient or in-patient care is available with 225 beds.
Ambulance service is also provided. The costs are reasonable.

Bumrungrad Hospital

33 Soi 3, Sukhumvit Rd.
Tel 02 667 1000   Fax 02 667 2525
community@bumrungrad.com
www.bumrungrad.com
This ultra-modern hospital is a favorite for both Thais and expats. It offers an extensive range of high-quality services and latest technologies. It is especially noted for a fully equipped and staffed ENT and Vision Centers. Helicopter ambulance service is available.

Piyavate Hospital

998 Rama IX Rd.
Tel 02 641 4499   Fax 02 246 9253
By appointment only. Excellent English spoken.

Samitivej Hospital

133 Soi 49, Sukhumvit Rd.
Tel 02 392 0011   Fax 02 391 1290
info@mail.samitivej.co.th
www.samitivej.co.th
This hospital provides ambulance service and the staff speaks English. The proficiency of the physicians and efficient procedures make it popular with expats who live in the Sukhumvit area.

Samitivej-Srinakarin Hospital

488 Srinakarin Rd.
Tel 02 731 7000   Fax 02 731 7044
nfo@mail.samitivej.co.th
Offers advanced technology for diagnosis and treatment. Especially good for out-patient care and doctor visits.

St. Louis Hospital

25 Sathorn Thai (South) Rd.
Tel 02 675 5000   Fax 02 675 5200.
www.saintlouis.or.th
This hospital specializes in dentistry, laser surgery, vision clinic, ear, nose and throat, urology, heart surgery, and gastrointestinal treatments.

Hospital Room Rates

The rates for a hospital stay are very reasonable. The Police Hospital (where accident victims are first taken), is the least expensive but the patients share a ward with no privacy.

All the private hospitals offer several forms of accommodation and service with private rooms available in most establishments. Here are the room and board rates for Samitivej Hospital and Bumrungrad Hospital. The exchange rate was 43 baht to the dollar (Jan 2003).

Samitivej and Bumrungrad hospitals are world-class institutions and their rates are slightly higher than others.

Samitivej Hospital Room Rates (baht per day)

Room type	Rate	Nursing	Service
VIP Room 1	4200	800	400
VIP Room 2	3500	800	400
Deluxe Room 1	3500	800	400
Deluxe Room 2	2900	800	400
Superior Room 1	2500	800	400
Superior Room 2	2200	800	300
Private Room 1	1700	800	300
Private Room 2	1500	800	300
ICU 1	4100	1600	400
ICU 2	3200	1600	400

Meals

Room Type	Cost Per Day
Thai food	350
Western food	480
Tube feeding	330
Liquid diet	250

Bumrungrad Hospital room Rates (baht per day)

Room type	Rate	Nursing	Service
Royal Suite	9000	1200	900
VIP Suite	6500	900	650
Single Deluxe	3500	850	350
Single Room	2400	800	240
2-bed Room	1100	530	110
4-bed Room	500	530	50
ICU	3400	2500	340

Meals

Room Type	Cost Per Day
Suite	460
Single Room	390
204 bed room	330
ICU	390

Samitivej Hospital

Bumrungrad Hospital

Pharmacies

Hospitals have dispensaries and there are hundreds of pharmacies throughout the city where medication can be purchased without a prescription.

These stores have pharmacies with English-speaking staff.

Foodland
Soi 5 Sukhumvit Rd.

Tops Marketplace
Soi 19 Sukhumvit Rd., at Robinson Dept. store.

Villa Supermarkets
Sukhumvit Rd., near the corner of Soi 33.

Dental Clinics

While living in Bangkok I visited dentists on a number of occasions for cleaning and fillings and have always been satisfied with their skill levels. Recently, I visited the dentist and had five fillings and teeth cleaned for $150.

The clinics listed below have gained solid reputations among the expat community. The doctors speak English and many have been trained and qualified in the US. Their specialties include restorative work, crowns, bridging, root canal.

Bangkok Adventist Mission Hospital
Dental Clinic Tel 02 282 1100

Bangkok General Hospital
Dental Center Tel 02 318 0066

Bumrungrad Hospital
Dental Clinic Tel 02 667 2300

Bangkok Nursing Hospital
Dental Clinic Tel 02 632 0560 Ext 1032

Dental Hospital

88/88 Soi 49 Sukhumvit Rd.
Tel 02 260 5000

Phya Thai Hospital

Dental clinic.
Tel 02 270 1830

Samitivej Hospital

Dental Clinic
Tel 02 392 0011 ext 1355

Health Insurance

BUPA Blue Cross

38 Q-house Convent Building
9th floor Convent Road,
Silom, Bangkok
Tel 02 234-7755
www.bupaThailand.com

AETNA OSOTSPA

Tel 02 651 4845   Fax 02 236 9375

Bangkok Life Assurance

Tel 02 203 0055   Fax 02 541 5545

Muang Thai Healthcare

Tel 02 276 1025   Fax 02 277 8391

Thai Health Insurance

Tel 02 246 9680   Fax 02 246 9806

Traditional Medicine

Besides western medicine, Bangkok has numerous venues for acupuncture and chiropractic treatments as well as massage and herbal remedies. As a writer without a disciplined exercise program I often get muscle cramps in my shoulders. I was writing a magazine article and pushing hard to meet the deadline when I noticed that my right shoulder was practically in my ear. The muscle was under tension. When it had happened before I had an acupuncturist that I had been going to but he had moved to Europe. His treatment was very efficient. It took only one visit each time during which he would interview me then insert a couple of needles in my shoulder muscle and one in the lower back After about 5 minutes he removed the needles and my shoulder was back to normal. Now I had to find a new acupuncturist.

From my Sukhumvit apartment I caught an air-conditioned bus to Chinatown and went to a herb shop on Yaowarat Road. A huge one with walls 15 feet high lined from floor to ceiling with what looked like letter boxes. Each one was labelled and clerks climbed ladders getting the boxes then bringing them to the counter where the apothecary selected a leaf from one, a bit of root from another and various other dried things, which he used to prepare the prescription.

Besides the appearance of the shop with its hundreds of boxes and various roots, leaves and herbs on display in the glass cases, the most overpowering sensation is the smell. It wasn't offensive, just a pungent, earthy aroma that you get when all these potent plants are put into one room. I went there since they would know of an acupuncturist, and they did. They told me of a man who hung his shingle in a nearby temple.

I found the temple easily enough, but wandered around the grounds for 15 minutes before I discovered the acupuncturist tucked away in an alcove. He was a slightly built, Chinese man in his sixties who carried the air of a competent healer though his open-air alcove was a light-year away from the air conditioned office of my last doctor. It was simply furnished with a wooden table and a couple of folding chairs.

He invited me to sit down, poured me a glass of iced *nam chaa*, and asked what was wrong. I told him about my shoulder problem. He squeezed it a couple of times, nodded knowingly and asked if I took any Western medicine. We talked for a while during which I found out that he was from Shanghai and had lived in Bangkok for 30 years. Then he showed me a sheaf of reference letters from foreigners that he had treated. They were convincing letters and didn't appear to be forged, so I said, okay, poke me with the needles. "Not here," he said, "we go to your house."

He got his case of needles, put a "Be back soon" sign on his desk and we left the temple.

"Let's take a cab," I said. It was only about a $5 fare.

"No. We take the bus."

At the bus stop I said, "Let's take the air-conditioned bus." A 25 cent fare.

"No. We take the regular bus." A seven cent ride.

We managed to get seats and 30 minutes later arrived at my apartment. I took off my shirt and he poked a couple of needles into the shoulder muscle and within minutes the shoulder dropped to its normal position and I could turn my head easily, which I couldn't do before.

"How much do I owe you?" I asked, not having any idea how much a house call might run.

"Oh, 200 or 250 baht," he answered politely. $8-10.

Several hospitals now provide a traditional healing center and acupuncturists are listed in the English edition of the yellow pages phone book.

Traditional Medicine Centers

BNH Hospital

Dr. Manee (lady doctor)
Tel 02 632 0560

Bodyology Center

Tel 02 662 6077
Soft laser therapy and Chinese acupuncture.

Siriraj Hospital

Tel 02641 7777
Acupuncture clinic.

Wat Po Traditional Medicine School of Thailand

Located in Wat Po
Patients are treated in the late afternoon.

Alcoholics Anonymous

The Rectory of the Holy Redeemer Church
123/19 Soi 5 Ruam Rudi
Tel 02 231 8300
Meetings every day. Call for times.

Women Only AA

The Rectory at Holy Redeemer Church
123/19 Soi 5 Ruam Rudi.
Tel 02 231 8300
Meetings Thursday 6:15 to 7:15 P.M.

Al-Anon Meetings

The Rectory at Holy Redeemer Church
123/19 Soi 5 Ruam Rudi.
Tel 02 256 6305
Call for meeting times.

Co-dependents Anonymous

Meetings in Rectory at Holy Redeemer Church
123/19 Soi 5 Ruam Rudi.
Tuesday 7 P.M. to 8 P.M.

Narcotics Anonymous

Call for meeting venue and times
Tel 02 256 6305

BNH Health Line

BNH Hospital 24-hour service
Tel 02 632 1000

Notes

125

Notes

City Life

In Bangkok, you'll probably never hear a police siren, witness a shoot-out, car chase or other sights and sounds of cops and robbers activities so familiar in American cities. Except for the occasional gold shop robbery or business rival assassination, crime involving guns and getaway motorcycles is a rare occurrence. What's more, Bangkok doesn't have areas where street crime goes with the territory and holdups, muggings, and rape are uncommon. Finally, since Thais rarely harbor, or at least display, feelings of racial or ethnic resentment it's very unlikely that you will be singled out because of prejudice.

You won't need to arm yourself for protection, in fact, it's not even a good idea. In all my travels throughout the kingdom, I carried only a Leatherman tool, and unless you are involved in an enemy-making activity, that's all you'll need. That's not to say that if you get drunk and flash a lot of cash you won't get rolled, or if you wear gold chains they won't get snatched. That can happen anywhere, but the chances are good that you won't be physically harmed. Traffic accidents are the most common, physical threats to life in the city. The key to avoiding them is caution and timing, not fear.

Traffic

Thais believe in karma and reincarnation, that they will not die before their time and then they will be reborn. This faith is clearly demonstrated in their driving style. Motorcycles race along at breakneck speed, weaving in and out of the traffic with only inches to spare. Vendors pushing noodle carts in the fast moving stream of traffic seem oblivious to the vehicles barely skimming by or dogging their heels. An American friend of mine calls Bangkok "The Land of The Close Shave." Here, how close people come to having an accident doesn't count. When one vehicle squeezes in front of another, that's okay. As a taxi driver explained it, "

He must belong there since he is there." Karma. You are where you are supposed to be or you wouldn't be there. At least that's the best I can figure it out. For the most part, the drivers remain courteous to each other, no hand or foot gestures, no cursing each other, no road rage attacks. When accidents do occur, drivers usually reach for their wallets, not their guns.

Bangkok's traffic jams are legendary. Rush hour streets can be chaotic and time consuming, but this problem has been greatly alleviated with the recent addition of the Skytrain that operates along the most heavily traveled roads. This service takes the place of many buses, a major source of traffic. To avoid the jams, plan your daytime excursions for the hours between 9 A.M. and 4 P.M. and in the evening hours after 7 P.M.

If you must be somewhere at a specified time, leave in plenty of time to get there. But when you are late for an appointment you will most often be excused since everyone knows how a seemingly simple, short journey has the potential to take a long time.

Don't lose your cool when crossing the streets. If a car passes within inches of you, don't get angry at the driver, he's long gone. Instead, feel grateful that you weren't hit. When you are engaged in negotiating traffic, anger is a luxury not a survival instinct. Don't hold hands with your significant other when crossing busy roads, independent action is safer.

Drivers will not automatically give pedestrians the right of way, even in marked crossing zones. The safest way to cross busy roads is by using the pedestrian overpass or crossing in a crowd, preferably alongside a pregnant woman. For some reason, Thai drivers give a lot of space to pregnant women.

When crossing the street, the drill is to look to your right, then left, then right again. Follow this rule even on one-way streets since motorcycles and buses often go against the traffic flow.

If, as a pedestrian, you are struck by a car, the driver is responsible for taking you to the hospital and paying the bill. This happened to me in a minor accident and the driver lived up to his obligation. But if for some reason this is not possible, take a taxi since getting an ambulance to the scene of an accident in a reasonable time is not always possible. There are hundreds of hospitals and clinics in the city so there is probably one within a mile or so of your location. Taxi drivers may refuse if you are bloody, and you may need to go by tuk-tuk.

As an unwritten rule, the ranking order of fault in an accident is determined by the size of the vehicles involved using the premise that the larger vehicle is at fault. A truck or bus that runs into a car is at fault. A car that runs into a tuk-tuk is at fault. A tuk-tuk that runs into a motorcycle or bicycle is at fault. Anything with wheels that runs into a pedestrian or an elephant is at fault.

Be especially alert when crossing at wide intersections equipped with traffic signals. During the red light, motorbikes filter through the cars to get as close to front rank as possible. When it changes to green they take off like it was a moto-cross event with dozens of machines going for the gold.

Street Smarts

While you probably won't meet with a weapon flashing robber you could be singled out by con artists, pickpockets, cutpurses, or grab-and-run thieves. This can happen to anyone, Thais included, so don't let anxiety run your life but take some precautions that will keep you out of trouble.

You will be approached by street touts offering "genuine" emeralds and rubies "smuggled" in from Burma at ridiculously low prices. Others hit on you with the lure of a card game. The games are rigged so that the house always wins. Even if you know that you have been cheated there's no recourse since gambling is illegal in Thailand. In the Sukhumvit Road and Silom Road areas, you may be approached by a man who quietly asks if you want a "massage" and discretely shows you a small, color brochure of the parlor and masseuses -- believe it or not, prostitution is illegal in Thailand. He will take you in his "taxi" but won't mention the exorbitant cost for his services until you want to leave the parlor. You will have to pay -- can't go to the police on this one.

Bangkok's night life is famous for its bustle, and infamous for its hustlers. On my first visit, I stayed at the Malaysia Hotel, a popular place with the backpacking set, of which I was a part. There was a bulletin board provided for the use of the guests where I read this message.

> *I want to warn everyone. Be careful when you go out with the Thai ladies. They are not to be trusted. They are thieves. I met two girls in a bar beer and took them to my hotel room. They told me to shower first. So I did, and when I came out they were running out the door, one was carrying my pants and the other one had my shoes. I chased them down the hall but since I was naked I went back to my room and discovered that they took all my money and my watch. These girls are thieves!*

Under this message someone scrawled, "Hey, chum, next time bring your mum."

There's no shame in being naive, but it can be harmful. Be cautious if you visit the "entertainment plazas," areas with beer bars and pole dancers favored by farangs. They are safe enough for the most part, and while you won't be robbed in the usual sense every effort will be made to separate you from your money. Some bars offer an exotic floor show, and "no cover charge" but the price of drinks is exorbitant and you won't get out without paying. Keep your radar tuned up for offers too good to be true, they probably are.

Most of the "rip-offs" you will experience will be of the overcharge and shortchange variety. Before you buy something, Always ask how much it is, *"Taorye, khrap?"* And always check the bills at restaurants and hotels, they are sometimes incorrect. But I can't say that the errors are on purpose since I've been undercharged as well as overcharged. Whenever you have a money problem like this, maintain your cool at all times. No threats, no heavy arguments. If it is a meaningful amount, call the Tourist Police.

Many newcomers to Bangkok are totally dazzled for the first few weeks by the abundance of gemstones for sale and it is on them that the Gem Scam is most effective.

One popular variation to this scam begins with a ride in a tuk-tuk when the driver tells you that your destination is closed for some reason. But you are in luck since the driver says that he is specially trained to be helpful to tourists. Then he mentions that the government has launched a promotion to sell gems to tourists, at very low prices.

If you show an interest, the tuk-tuk driver will drive around until you " accidentally" meet a well-dressed young man or an older, distinguished man. The younger man says he is a student while the older one will claim he works for the government and shows you his (counterfeit) government ID. This person confirms the "government gems sales" story.

If you take the bait and go to the "government" jewelry store you are told that it's possible to make 100-150% profit by reselling the gems back home. As a final touch, the seller writes a vague guarantee like "if everything is not perfect we will offer a full refund" and puts an official looking stamp on it. Later you discover that the gems were nowhere near the value you were told. There is very little recourse for recovering your money.

"Genuine antiques" is another scam to be wary of. Skilled craftsmen can make a reproduction appear to be as old as dirt. A friend from Hawaii visited me on his first visit to Bangkok. He was a self assured fellow but had never been traveling before and was ready for picking. Fortunately for him, he only got slightly plucked.

He returned to my apartment after a day of exploring the city wearing a smug, "I got a good deal" look on his face.

"Have I got something to show you," he said as he pulled a small bag from his day pack. He smiled as he shook the bag making a clinking sound. Then he upended the bag and poured a pile of coins on a table.

"Check this out," he said.

They were of different sizes and, covered with a heavy patina and encrusted mud, appeared to be very old.

"I was walking on Sukhumvit when I saw this old man sitting on a blanket with a pile of these coins all covered with mud. He had a pan of water next to him and he was washing the coins. They obviously had been dredged up from the river or one of the canals. I don't think the old man knew what they were worth. He sold me this bag full for twenty dollars. These are collector's coins!"

Two things were wrong with my friend's assumptions. First of all, he knew nothing about rare coins, and secondly, he didn't know that there were dozens of these "coin men" in Bangkok. All selling the same way, on a blanket with a pile of muddy coins and a wash basin, and acting very naÔve. What's more they all buy their coins from the rare-coin makers in Chinatown.

Be wary, not afraid. The great majority of Thais are friendly, polite and helpful, and are ready to return a smile. On your city walks you will pass many street vendors who will smile and ask, "Where you go," as an icebreaker phrase. A common answer is, "just for a walk," or "*by thio*" which means " out for fun." Many Thais speak a little English and want to try it out, giving you an opportunity to make acquaintances. If you are friendly, polite and outgoing you will have little trouble meeting Thais and although you may not understand each other's language you will be on safe ground if you acknowledge them with a smile. Don't divulge too much of your personal life. Keep the conversation on general topics. You can control its course by asking the questions. "Are you from Bangkok?" "Where did you learn English?" "Is it always this hot?" Friendly bargaining is another way to make acquaintances. You don't need to buy anything. Thais make friends easily and after a few weeks you should know a few people that you trust not to give you a bum steer.

Bangkok's expat community is made up of people from Europe, Africa, the Middle East, Russia, China, Australia, and all parts of Asia. Don't get the idea that just because someone is the same race or color, or nationality as yours that they will be honest with you. The latest wave of scamsters are Russian prostitutes and gangsters but all the other nationalities are fairly represented.

Police

When Americans talk about police corruption in Thailand their opinions are based on the judicial systems of their homeland where citations are issued for misdemeanor crimes, and the accused are given the opportunity to pay the fine or appear in court. In Thailand a person charged with a misdemeanor can either pay the fine to the arresting officer or go to jail, go to court, and then pay the fine. Since the judicial system is based on the French model where you are guilty until proven innocent, there's only a remote chance you will win the case. It's best to pay the fine on the spot since the more people that are involved, the more it costs. The good news is that the fine is negotiable.

For example, on a recent trip to Bangkok I was standing near the bus stop at the corner of Sukhumvit and Soi 4 (Nana) when without thinking I dropped a candy wrapper on the ground. A few seconds later, a young policeman wearing a custom fitted, brown uniform and a cap with a high peak like a German Army officer's, came up to me and pointed to the ground. I immediately realized what he meant and gave an embarrassed smile as I picked up the wrapper. He indicated with a slight motion of his hand to follow him. We walked up Sukhumvit one block to his post, a small, open-air police kiosk

on Soi 2. There he pointed to a sign board printed in Thai and English stating that littering was a 2000 baht fine. He went into the kiosk and I walked over to face him. He gave me a brochure with the littering law spelled out in Thai and English and the 2000 baht in large, red letters.

"You understand?" He asked in English.

I answered in Thai, "*Khaochai, khrap*," I understand, sir.

He shuffled some papers, brought out his pen and stalled as he thought it over then said, "The fine is 2000 baht. Or a favorable amount."

I took my time in answering, looking deep in thought, then said, " *Sawng loy baht*, okay?" Two hundred baht, okay? Every Thai understands "okay".

He took his time in answering, rubbed his chin, rustled the papers on the desk, then looked up at me. "Okay. Sawng loy baht." I took the money off my clip as he reached for a small book, "Do you want a receipt?" He asked in English.

"No, thank you. I don't need one." What for? To write off on my taxes? I don't care what happens to the money after I give it to him. It's less than US $5.

Some people say this encourages police corruption. Maybe it does but what are the options in this or in any similar encounter with the police? I want to see your chief? I want to call the American Embassy? I find it very easy to live in a country where you can pay a policeman to leave you alone.

Contrary to popular belief, the fine increases as you go up the chain of command. Your best deal is the first one you can make. Forget the call to the Embassy, you'll get no back-up from them. One last note of caution, if you insist on seeing the officer's superior you may be taken there, hands cuffed behind your back, sandwiched between two cops on the seat of a 125 cc Yamaha motorcycle. Police don't use patrol cars in Bangkok.

Sometimes the police will set up checkpoints on busy roads and pull over cars and motorcycles at random. Practically every vehicle ends up paying a "fine" whether they did something illegal at that moment or not. "That's a shakedown," cry the farang motorists, "I didn't do anything wrong!" Maybe not then, but there's not a driver in Bangkok who isn't guilty of a couple of dozen illegal turns, or other slight infractions. It's pay up time. Bargain!

This method of fine collection doesn't give all the money to the arresting officer. He's the collector of fines and has to pipe some of it up the chain. These fines increase his income, those of his superiors and the department in general. Cops in Thailand are not overpaid. I have met several policemen while teaching English and they explained their side of the story. Their method of fine collection may not agree with your morals and ethics but it works here.

Certainly there are abuses of this system but there is no police force in the world that is not corrupt to one degree or another. In the US, people have had cars and houses confiscated immediately, on the mere suspicion, not conviction, of drug dealing. Then, in some cases these assets are not returned even though the party was proven innocent, instead they go directly to the arresting agency to fund their activities. There have been reports of Thai policemen shaking-down farangs on real or trumped up charges and the usual drill is to coerce them to making cash withdrawals from an ATM machine to pay the "fine."

It probably occurs, but in 12 years of living in Thailand I've never heard a first-hand story or witnessed police brutality. The police don't want blood, they want money. If you go along without resistance, you will probably not be harmed. My first observation of police activities took place at the old Atlanta Hotel on Soi 2 Sukhumvit. I arrived in town from Chiang Mai one morning and went to the hotel at the dead end of the soi. As I approached I saw three shiny black, pickup trucks on the street and a large semi-circle of armed soldiers watching the entrance. As I got closer, I could hear yelling from inside the hotel. An unsmiling soldier who had been watching me approach signaled me over to him. He motioned for me to put my backpack on the ground and indicated that I should open it. He gave it a cursory search then nodded to indicate that he was finished. I closed the pack and stood there waiting for more directions.

I gave him a palm up sign and looked at the hotel as if to ask, "What's going on?" He just smiled, shook his head and said, "*My pen rai.*" Never mind. I soon realized it was a drug raid as an occasional farang, not handcuffed and not even being held onto by his captors, was escorted out of the building and seated in a truck. There was no shoving, nobody was up against the wall with arms outstretched and legs spread, with guns shoved into their necks, and no one was being beaten. The police spoke in normal tones, the yelling was from the hotel residents, and went about their job without fuss, blood, or bullets. They collected about ten people, loaded the soldiers up and left without sirens or even screeching tires.

Another police incident I witnessed occurred in a bar where a big, German man had drunk too much and became threatening to the bartender and the Thai girls who worked there. After awhile a cop was called and he tried to get the German to leave peacefully, but the man wasn't through ranting and was beating his fist on the bar while swearing at the bartender. The cop simply grabbed the man's wrist and pressed his finger onto the pressure point and in a moment the German was buckling at the knees. The cop led him outside and let him go. The German took the hint and willingly moved on, rubbing his wrist.

There are police kiosks at many of the major intersections and other locations in the city. Only rarely will you see a police car since street patrols are done by motorcycle, two cops on a 125 cc Yamaha.

There are two Police Departments, the regular police, and the Tourist Police. The Tourist Police have a limited jurisdiction but unlike the regular police, the officers speak English. Unless you have an interpreter with you, call them first in an emergency and ask for assistance in contacting the regular police.

Non-Prejudicial Society

Thais are very cordial towards Americans. Often, when I tell a new acquaintance that I'm American, they will say something like, "America number one" and give the thumbs-up sign. Other nationalities may get this response as well, I don't know. But then America has always had an amiable relationship with the kingdom without making territorial or unfair trade demands.

Much of this goodwill may stem from World War Two when at the end of the war Britain petitioned to require Thailand to pay huge war reparations because the government had not resisted the Japanese, but America vetoed the motion. Then, during the Vietnam War hundreds of thousands of American servicemen were stationed or visited the kingdom and thousands of Thais worked on US bases. Whatever the reason, Thai people have no apparent animosity or resentments against Americans in general.

I lived in Bangkok during the Gulf War working for an advertising company as a copywriter. One of my accounts was a travel agency owned by an Iraqi woman in her forties. We had been friends since before the war and I wondered if our relationship would change. I have no prejudice against any country, race or religion. Not to say that I never had prejudices but a few years of travel has removed them. At our next meeting, her views of the war were focused on her anxieties for her parents who lived in Baghdad which was then being seriously bombed. Our friendship was strengthened by our shared fear for her family.

Whatever religion Thais follow, they are still Thais and essentially conform to the social customs of the kingdom, especially courtesy and the avoidance of confrontation. The rare, anti-American resentment often comes from other farangs. Expats in Bangkok often behave like sailors on liberty: Go to a bar, get drunk and discuss politics and national pride.

I spent 7 weeks in Thailand, from late October to the first week of December 2002 and split the time between Bangkok and Phuket. Bangkok is still very safe for Americans although last year there were vague reports of harassment on Soi 3 Sukhumvit. This area has many Muslim restaurants and is popular with middle-eastern people. It's unclear who instigated the situations, Americans or Muslims, since there is an "entertainment plaza" across the street that is popular with expats.

Keep in mind that while most Americans can't distinguish the differences among a Sikh, a Hindu, a Muslim, or anyone who wears a beard and turban, so do Eastern people have difficulty distinguishing Westerners. Americans, Brits, Canadians, Australians, Danes, Germans and other Europeans all look the same to them. Until you disclose your nationality, people can only guess where you are from. It's highly unlikely that anyone is out to get Americans in Bangkok. Use your street smarts and you will avoid trouble.

Register with the US Embassy in Bangkok and keep up to date on the safety issues in the kingdom by Email. Here is a bulletin that was sent by the Embassy to US citizens living in Thailand.

The Embassy Warning

To: American wardens and other American citizens in Thailand

From: US Embassy Bangkok

SUBJECT: Security Precautions

All of us have been touched by the outpouring of sympathy and support from the Thai people. However, we must not overlook the fact that Bangkok is a major tourist point and one of the world's largest international cities. We need to be aware that some individuals transiting, visiting, or living in Thailand may have very strong feelings that conflict with ours.

While most with such views remain courteous, the Embassy's Security Office has received a few reports of harassment of Westerners by individuals opposed to the US policy in the wake of the terrorist attacks. Although there have been no incidents of violence or injury, emotions could continue to rise as the US response to terrorism takes shape over the next several days, weeks, and months.

The Royal Thai Police is providing continued excellent support, but it is important to practice good security and avoid potential trouble when and wherever we can.

In this regard, the following security measures are recommended:

√ *Maintain a low profile. Avoid wearing distinctively 'American' garb.*

√ *Avoid demonstrations of any kind. If you see one forming or coming toward you, leave the area immediately.*

√ *Ignore anti-American taunts or verbal comments if encountered, and leave the area immediately.*

√ *While in your car, keep the windows up and the doors locked. If you are harassed while stopped at a red light or in traffic, remain calm, ignore the source of the harassment and leave the area as soon as possible. If you are followed, stop the first policeman you see, or drive to a police station or other location of safety. Notify the police immediately, by cell phone if you have one.*

√ *Avoid becoming involved in arguments over U.S. policy with strangers, and break off conversations with those who insist on discussing controversial topics in a threatening manner.*

√ *Should you observe obvious signs of anti-American sentiment, such as windows displaying pictures of Osama Bin Laden or anti-American posters, leave the area immediately.*

One particular area you should be aware of is the Soi 3, Nana area where a few of the harassment complaints we have received have taken place. When you pass through this area, please be particularly mindful of your surroundings and those around you.

Should you encounter any harassment at all, or observe areas that you think should be avoided because of anti-American sentiments, please notify the police immediately. Also, please report any incidents or observations to the Embassy's American Citizen Services Unit. The Email address is acsbkk@state.gov and the telephone number is +66 (0) 2205-4049. We will continue to keep you updated as information is received.

Note:

One way to avoid problems with anyone who doesn't like Americans is to claim to be a Canadian. Everyone likes them and the speech accent is easy to learn. Otherwise, update your street smarts along with a courteous attitude towards everyone and use your best judgement as to when to express your political opinions. Bangkok is still a very safe city since the basic goal of the inhabitants whether Buddhist, Muslim, Christian, Taoist, or Sikh, is to make a living, not an enemy.

Notes

Notes

Social Customs

Thai social life is regulated not only by recorded laws but also by unwritten customs, and even though the population of the kingdom has several ethnic groups and various religions, the customs of the Thai people are the accepted norm.

In most cases, offending these customs will only cause you to lose some social "face." The Thais will give you some slack for your ignorance, but offenses against the religion or royal family are taken very seriously. On the island of Ko Samui, a French couple were surrounded by angry villagers when they were discovered posing on a statue of Buddha while taking photos. The Tourist Police showed up in time to save the couple from serious harassment, and then fined them.

While the observance of social customs is taken seriously by Thais, farangs (Westerners) sometimes balk at the idea. I have no problem adopting the ways of Thais. A couple of them open a new dimension of peace and togetherness.

Twice each day, at 8 A.M. and 6 P.M. the National Anthem is played over the radio and television stations as well as through loudspeakers at government offices and schools. In small towns and villages, vehicles stop where they are and pedestrians stand respectfully. It's over in a couple of minutes and life picks up where it left off, like a freeze frame in a movie. Stopping the flow of traffic in Bangkok at these hours is not feasible, though much of it is already involuntarily stalled, but Thais everywhere stop what they're doing and reaffirm their commitment to the nation. I knew one senior citizen who snapped to attention, ramrod straight, chest out, stomach in, chin tucked like a drill sergeant's, eyes focused ahead -- and this was in his house.

The Royal Anthem honoring the monarchy is played before sports events, plays, concerts, and everyone stands in silence until it is over. Movie theaters play the anthem and show pictures of the royal family inspecting government projects, establishing health and education services and providing welfare to the people. The entire audience rises when the music begins.

At one theater, I was seated behind a blond haired fellow and a Thai girl who appeared to be on a first date. Smiles, eye contact, occasional attempts at communication. When the audience stood up for the Royal Anthem she noticed that her boyfriend was still seated. When she urged him to stand up he said in a loud voice, "I don't stand for no man!" No one turned to look at him. They probably didn't care whether he stood up or not, but the girl was no doubt embarrassed by his rudeness. A few minutes after the movie started she left her seat and didn't return.

You are not required by law to observe these unwritten rules of social conduct but trying your best not to violate them will certainly enhance your life in Thailand. Even clumsy and inept attempts to follow them will earn you respect and esteem from the people you come into contact with. You are not giving up anything by adhering to these customs, instead you are gaining the knowledge of a different way of life. That's what living in Thailand is all about.

The interpretations of social customs given here come from research as well as my own experiences. This list is not a full index but a selection that will smooth your entry into Thai society. Over the years, I made a lot of Thai friends and joined them on excursions to their home villages where farangs rarely went. I was stared at from doorways, followed by children, and required to greet everyone I met, whether we understood each other or not.

Thai men greet people with a *wai* and say, "*Sa wat dee, khrap.*" Thai women wai and say, "*Sa wat dee, ka.*" *Sa wat dee* means good day, good evening , good night and good-bye. *Khrap* or *ka* is the customary, respectful conversation tag. The next question varies among "How are you?" "Where are you going?" "Have you eaten, yet?"

When departing, Thais will wai and say, "*Sa wat dee, khrap (ka),*" and sometimes back up a step or two before starting off. Another common departure phrase is, *"Chok dee, khrap (ka),"* good luck. Always end statements or questions with the respectful modifiers *khrap* or *ka* no matter who you are talking to.

The Thai people are very unified since their social fabric has not been torn by civil war and the kingdom has never been colonized by foreign nations. Another unifying thread is that the overwhelming majority of Thais are Buddhists and involve themselves fully and cooperatively in the maintenance of their religion on a daily basis.

Then too, Thais are customarily involved in community projects from an early age. They help with chores around the village, tending buffalo, harvesting rice or preparing food, and school projects don't leave anyone off of the duty roster. In the provinces, it's common for the schoolchildren to pitch in on the maintenance and repair of their school. This includes cleaning the toilets, clearing weeks, planting flowers, and any other tasks within their capabilities. It's here that Thais form the discipline, teamwork, and respect for authority they need to bond effectively with their society.

The 'Wai'

Shaking a person's hand when being introduced or meeting them is not the Thai way and most of them fumble uncomfortably with this Western custom. The handshake is said to have originated as a way to show the person you were meeting that you had no weapons in your hand.

The traditional Thai greeting is the *wai*, and although it has been compared to the western handshake, it implies much more. The wai signifies respect to the person to whom it is given. It is made by putting your palms together and placing your index fingertips on your chin, nose or forehead and bowing your head slightly. Each location marks different degrees of respect, the higher the position of the hands the more respect that is being given.

Knowing when to wai and when to shake hands can be confusing. Sometimes you will meet a Thai who has lived in the West and as you raise your wai he's extending his hand for a handshake. Then you will switch roles a couple of times and have a laugh when you finally coordinate your greetings.

For the most part you will be better off to use the wai as your greeting to adults, but don't wai maids, service people, or children until they wai you first. A wai is always given first by the person who is lower in the social order than the person being waied. This "class" system may offend expatriates who believe in equality among people but it works here. To ignore this rule will embarrass the person waied to. To kids or service personnel, a nod of the head and a smile is sufficient.

Thais naturally take the social measure of people they meet, including farangs, and it is this factor that determines who wais first. Anyone going into a government office on business will wai the officers first.

When someone wais to you, return the gesture since not to do so would be like refusing a handshake, or worse. When someone wais to you first it indicates that the person regards you as superior to them and not to wai in return would be a social snub. There will be times when, for various reasons, you will be unable to return the wai, this is excused as long as you acknowledge the gesture with a greeting, a nod of the head, a smile or even the lifting of a little finger.

Foreigners should not initiate a wai to those that would be considered occupationally inferior. Don't wai tradesmen, domestic help, waiters or taxi drivers even if you are younger than they, until they wai you first. When you are paying for service you are the boss and bosses don't wai first.

Mai pen rai

Mai pen rai means "it's okay," "never mind," "no problem." Thais will say it when you thank them for doing you a favor, apologize for stepping on someone's toes in a crowded bus, spill something on the table, or whine about missing your travel connections. It resolves or defuses personal encounters and greatly helps in keeping the stress level down. But some Westerners may have trouble accepting this easy attitude since they are used to a more emotional response.

Once, while on my way to a business appointment I was stuck in traffic and my frustration showed on my facial expressions and body language while the taxi driver said only , "Mai pen rai. We will get there." "But you don't understand," I said, "I'm late!" Then when I showed up at the appointment an hour late, apologizing profusely, the person I met with said, "Mai pen rai. You are here now," and sincerely meant it -- no problem. I wasted a couple of hours that day feeling anxious and impatient over something I could do nothing about.

After adopting this philosophy for myself I found it very calming in situations that were beyond my control. After all, what are the options? Angry frustration or calm acceptance, which do you want? But don't mistake this as total surrender to the fates. The Mai Pen Rai method removes negative thoughts about the situation and allows you to become part of the solution, not the problem.

Jai yen

This literally means "cool heart", but customarily it means "Keep your cool. Don't lose your temper." The chances are that you will rarely have an opportunity to say this to a Thai person, but you will find it very useful to repeat it to yourself, over and over like a mantra when you are becoming angry or impatient at something or someone. This technique has saved me many times from opening mouth and inserting foot, saying something I wish I hadn't. Absolutely nothing positive is accomplished by displays of anger, whether it's a loud tirade or a silent scowl.

No one is perfect and Thais sometimes express their displeasure at situations or people, but for the most part they are very self controlled. It is the Middle Way to back away from a confrontation rather than to escalate it. But don't mistake this stance as timidity or servility. Thais can become as angry and resentful as anyone else and might take the opportunity to express it covertly. Don't insult or demean the waiter who has control over your food. Revenge is an acceptable ego salve.

Since physical confrontation is the last resort Thais use warnings as another way to avenge their honor when someone berates or demeans them. I once worked as an advisor for a Swedish tour boat company in Pattaya. The owner, a man in his forties had married a Thai and over a few years became a moderately successful exporter to Europe and owned upscale guest houses in Bangkok and Pattaya. The tour boat company was just being organized and the boat was still on dry land being fitted out. The work went slowly and the owner was getting more impatient each day.

One day he lost his temper with one of the crew that was working on the boat. The man had come to work drunk and was causing disruptions. After a couple of hours working in the 100 degree heat the owner let him have it with both barrels, western style. "You're useless! You're drunk! You're fired! Get off the property!" The man became stone quiet. His face frozen into a nobody-talks-to-me-like-that glare. He looked around at his crew on the boat. They averted his glance, you don't look at a person who has just lost face in front of you. Then he settled his gaze on the owner. The man looked like a South China Seas pirate. A red cloth tied snugly on his head, his dusky Southern Thai face glistening with sweat, and his red, white and ebony eyes doing their best to laser the life out of the pink Swede who insulted him. Finally he climbed off the boat and left the yard. The next day, the owner received a phone call telling him he had better leave Pattaya. He immediately left for Bangkok and did not return. He had been in the country long enough to take the advice seriously.

Jai yen is the rule of the day. Keep your cool at all times. That's not to say that you can't defend yourself when you are physically threatened, but be absolutely certain that you are being threatened, not simply teased, taunted or goaded. Thailand is a place where everything you learned in anger management classes pays off. Here, outward displays of anger are not only unacceptable, they can cost you money.

For a couple of years my wife and I belonged to a yacht club in Chonburi at the head of the Gulf of Thailand, an hour's bus ride from Bangkok. The bus would drop us off on Sukhumvit Road near Chonburi and from there we took motorcycle taxis to the club where we spent the day. When we departed in the afternoon, the manager, a retired Brit, had his driver take us back to Sukhumvit Road where he would flag down a Bangkok bound bus.

One afternoon, the driver, my wife, and I stood on the shoulder of the road. He was checking the buses as they approached to see their destination signs when a bus pulled onto the shoulder and came to a stop near us. " This one?" I asked him. "No," he said. The front door of the bus opened and a hefty Chinese-Thai man got out and walked towards us. He walked straight up to our driver and began talking in very angry tones. That got my attention and I watched as the man strengthened his tone and stepped towards our driver forcing him to back up. Then the man slapped our driver, berated him for a few more seconds, got back on the bus and left. The shame the driver felt was visible on his face, what was left of it after losing so much in front of us and a bus load of passengers.

The following week we went to the club and were talking with the manager when he said, "Oh, you remember the incident last week when my driver was slapped? Well, the police got the fellow. When my man returned he called the police and reported it. It was a private matter. Anyway, the police radioed ahead and stopped the bus forty miles from here and fined the man 500 baht. The fine for fighting starts at 500 baht, and if my man had hit back, he would have been fined as well. That's the way it is in Thailand."

If you fight with a Thai, the chances are that nearby people will jump on you, regardless of who is right or wrong, and if you get into a fight in a bar or other public place, you will pay for the property damage.

Patience

Thais are incredibly patient. They can absorb several hours of waiting in traffic jams, or in a bus that has broken down in the heat of the day, without a whimper. One time I boarded the train in Bangkok for Chiang

Mai. It was due to leave at 3:30 P.M. but because of an accident along the line 20 miles out of the city, it didn't leave until noon the next day. Men women and children lived together, without complaint, many of them on the hard seats in third class. One man I talked to summed up his feelings, " Good thing it happened while we are still in the station where there is plenty to eat and drink." For the most part, your patience will be required in minor matters like waiting for service in a restaurant, or for someone to show up for an appointment.

Tolerance

This is a well developed virtue among the Thais, how else would they be able to accept the multitude of social blunders that are committed by farangs. Except in situations where a person has offended the monarchy or religion, Thai people excuse all manner of mistakes by assuming that farangs don't know any better.

Farangs on the other hand, are not so quick to grant this pardon. They come from countries where companies are expected to have efficient staff trained to "multi-tasking" and be quick about it, but Thais are not geared like that and resist any attempts to change them. You will need to stretch your limits of tolerance to fit in. Be especially forgiving, but never condescending, over perceived shortcomings of people you come into contact with. Never degrade their efforts to serve you whether the person is an executive of a company or the janitor. Treat everyone with respect.

147

Cultural Caveats

√ Use the polite form of address, *Khun*, when addressing or referring to any adult Thai. Men should use the social softener, *khrap*, (*a* as in *fa*) and women say *ka* at the ends of your statements or questions. For example, "Sawatdee khrap, Khun Wilat." Good day, Mister Wilat. "Khun sabai dee mai, khrap?" You are well, no? "Khab khun, khrap." Thank you. Use these words even when you are speaking English with a Thai. "Sawatdee, khrap, Khun Wilat. Have you seen Khun Oy?" This respectful approach towards Thais will greatly smooth your dealings with every person you meet whether beggars, bar girls or bankers, and they will respect you in turn.

√ Don't express feelings of fondness in public. Touching, hugging, kissing in public is considered vulgar. Even after a long separation, public meetings between loved ones are made with respectful wais, flower garlands, and small talk in a normal tone. (Jai yen)

√ To signal someone to come to you, extend your right hand, palm down, and move your fingers up and down.

√ Don't whistle, clap or wave your arms to signal a waiters or other service people, use the "come here" hand signal.

√ Don't be offended if, after you have done a favor for, or presented a gift to a Thai there is only a slight indication of gratitude. (Jai yen)

√ Don't be too profuse when expressing your gratitude for a favor or gift. A sincere "thank you" and a respectful wai is enough. (Jai yen)

√ Don't be upset if your verbal instructions are forgotten or not followed. The staff in restaurants have a difficult time interpreting food orders from farangs and often ask you to repeat your request. (Patience and tolerance)

√ Don't be surprised when Thais are late for appointments. They wouldn't hold it against you if you were late or didn't show up at all. (Mai pen rai)

√ Don't expect Thais to feel the same sense of urgency or responsibility towards your problems or situations as you do. (Jai yen)

√ Don't judge actions or customs as wrong simply because they offend your sensitivities, morals or ethics. (Tolerance)

√ Don't judge Thailand using Bangkok as the rule. Any nation's capital is the behavioral exception. Accept the best and leave the rest. (Tolerance)

√ Don't believe that every time a Thai answers yes to a question, that they mean yes. Yes can mean no, as well. This is caused by a grammatical mix up in the way a question is framed, as well as the Thai reluctance to say no to a request. Some second guessing will be required to get approximately the correct answer. (Tolerance)

√ Be very respectful when you are in temple grounds, near a statue of Buddha, or any other obviously revered location. Don't climb on the statues or structures.

√ Although the weather is hot and muggy, very few Thais wear shorts or go around shirtless. It's a city, not a resort and nothing marks you as a tourist or a newcomer quicker than the way you dress.

√ The Thais regard your appearance as an indicator of your class as well as a mark of respect shown to them. If you go to a government office wearing shorts, tee shirt and sandals you will still be served but your casual appearance may be resented.

√ Thai women dress very modestly and western women will avoid rude experiences if they do the same. Off the shoulder blouses, see-through material or other forms of provocative clothing are generally only worn by prostitutes, Thai or Western.

√ Don't speak in a loud voice unless necessary. It sends signals of displeasure whether or not you intend them.

Body Talk

Unlike hand shaking, back slapping, shoulder patting, hair tousling, bear hugging Americans, Thais are not a touchy-feely society. Except in emergencies, they don't like to touch or be touched without permission. Even policemen making an arrest will not touch the accused unless it becomes necessary.

Casual touches between people, especially between men and women, should not be made. It may be excused between same sex persons if it is a spontaneous, reflexive action followed by an apology, *"kaw toht, khrap,"* but it is not so easily forgiven if it occurs between a man and a women. Thais follow this custom so farangs are the usual offenders, men more often than women. A man who makes advances to a woman by casual touching is asking for trouble.

The Head

While Thais may adopt a grin-and-bear-it attitude for accidental body contact, they almost never tolerate their heads being touched without permission.

Don't touch anyone's head for any reason, no matter how young they are. Thais consider the head as the most sacred part of the body and the rules for offending this sensitivity are strictly observed. If there is something on a person's head, say a fallen leaf, you may ask permission to remove it. Otherwise, keep your hands out of their hair.

The Feet

As the head is the most sacred part of the body, the feet are the least and not knowing the rules of body language regarding them can cause you a lot of trouble.

Keep your feet flat on the floor when sitting down. It is very disrespectful to accidently face the soles of your feet, with or without shoes, directly at a person, a religious object or a portrait of the Royal Family. When done on purpose, it means "you are lower than the bottom of my foot," an extreme insult to a proud Thai. "Do you want to see my foot?" is the Thai invitation for a fight. A British friend of mine learned about this one harrowing night in Chiang Mai.

"I was in a samlor (a three-wheeled bicycle taxi used in the provinces), when, at an intersection, a large truck came roaring up towards us from the right side. I was apprehensive that it would not stop in time and extended my leg towards it to indicate, "Whoa!" At least that's what it means in Britain. The samlor driver saw my action and began pedaling like mad as the truck suddenly turned in behind us, grinding gears and picking up speed. It was late at night and there was no traffic and through all the turns the samlor driver took the snarling truck stayed right on our tail flashing the high beams. I recognized road rage and was relieved when the samlor turned into a housing compound, but the truck followed right behind. The samlor driver got out and began waiing to the truck driver who left the lights on and the motor running as he got out and walked towards me, shaking his fist and yelling. I didn't know whether to stay in the samlor or get out. I couldn't imagine what I had done to make the driver so angry at me! Fortunately, some of the people who lived in the compound heard the commotion and came out to investigate. They succeeded in calming the driver and a man told me that I had shown the bottom of my foot to him. How was I to know that was an invitation to fight?"

Never put your feet on tables, desks, chairs or prop them against the backs of theater or transportation seats.

Shoes or socks should never be stored overhead. On one train ride, there was a great commotion in my car caused when a European traveler placed his Doc Martin boots in the overhead luggage rack. But while the Thais would not touch the boots they ranted at the conductor until the owner took them down.

The Hands

Thailand, like other Asian countries, regards the right hand as the acceptable one to use at meals and in social settings. The left hand is the one used for cleaning oneself after using the toilet.

Use only your right hand when receiving or offering gifts. Left handed people are not excused from this custom. Although you might never notice it, there are many left-handed people in Thailand who have trained themselves in this custom. In Old Asia, a thief's right had was cut off as punishment, not only did it slow down his thieving, but also excluded him from the community rice bowl where people ate with their hands, right hands only.

When receiving something from an elderly person or one of senior or official status, take it with your right hand and place your left hand in a supporting position under your right elbow. Even in less esteemed situations, say a shopkeeper is handing you your purchases, he will often give you the package this way. This action conveys thanks, respect and humility. When someone is handing you something, accept it gracefully, never snatch something out of another persons hand.

Never point your finger at anyone, especially in anger. When you need to indicate a person use motions of your head and eyes. Use hand motions when giving directions.

The Body

Never step over any part of another person. This can become a test of diplomacy and balance on a train where sleeping people extend their legs into the aisles.

It is considered disrespectful even to walk over animals as I found out when I stepped over a sleeping dog and the Thai people nearby moaned collectively and looked at me in alarm.

In Thai Homes

No matter how humble or regal it is, a Thai's home is his palace and certain customs are always observed.

√ Remove your shoes before entering a house. Like all Asians, Thais have adopted the practice of not wearing shoes in the house. This is a health custom since Thais sit, sleep and even eat on the floor. In rural areas it is even more important since people work on farms where dirt borne diseases are always a problem. If you don't want to leave your Guccis outside the door, ask your host if you may have some paper to place them on inside. Even if your friend says it's okay to wear your shoes in the house, don't do it. This is one time when "yes" means "no."

In Myanmar (Burma), Thailand's neighbor, "no" means "no" as the British found out after they annexed the country. In 1824 the relations between Britain and Burma boiled over in the Second Anglo-Burmese War called "The Shoe Question," caused by the British refusal to remove their shoes when entering a house.

√ Don't step on the threshold. This is the bottom section of the door frame. Step over it. This rule applies to all door frames. For me, the "no shoes" rule was easier to remember and I violated this one a number of times before it was committed to memory.

√ Sit where you are told. Your host will indicate where you are to sit, and this becomes your place during the visit. Always return to it.

√ Don't wander around the house or presume to know where the toilet is and go looking for it on your own. Ask your host if you may use the toilet and he will show you the way.

√ Don't wear all black or all white clothing, these are colors for funerals. Although your hosts will not say anything if you do they may give you some questioning looks, wondering who died.

In The Workplace

While Thai customs are vital in the workplace, equally important to understand are the Thai attitudes concerning co-worker relationships and harmony.

For many Westerners, some of these attitudes are in direct opposition to their training, experience, or management style. Some expatriates adapt quickly to the Thai ways. Others take more time. But, eventually they all discover the Thai ways of working together.

Sanook

√ For Thais, a workplace must have an attitude of sanook (enjoyment, fun) or they quit. They don't go to the boss and complain. They simply come up with an excuse and quit. The job was no longer sanook. It may be their problem. Perhaps they will never find jobs they like. But if several employees quit in a relatively short period, it's probably because the work is *mai sanook* (not fun).

√ Maintain an upbeat attitude, or at least, the appearance of one. Thais are automatic smilers and to not return a smile is seen as a signal of displeasure. It doesn't need to be big. A slight grin and a nod of the head will do.

√ If you have problems with a coworker, employee or supervisor do not lose your temper or directly confront them in front of other staff members. To do so would cause the person to lose face. Keep your differences private and polite.

√ Never put up the front, "If I can do it, so can you."

√ Don't hold meetings on Saturdays.

√ Don't be a timekeeping tyrant. If a meeting is delayed because a person is late, let it pass without comment.

√ Accept the hospitality of co-workers when they offer you snacks.

√ Memorize the names of your co-workers.

√ Make every effort to communicate clearly. Nothing breaks the sanook feeling quicker or more thoroughly than confusing instructions.

Festivals

One nice thing about living in Thailand is that you get three new years: the Western New Year in January, Chinese New Year in February, and the Thai New Year in April. Until 1940, Thailand's New Year began on April 13 of the Western calendar, then it was changed to January 1 for the convenience of agreement with Western nations. Even so, the original New Year's Day is still a major holiday season called Songkran, The Water Festival.

This is the hottest time of the year and a water festival is fitting. The major activity of this occasion involves people pouring, squirting, or throwing water on each other. The origins of this custom are not clear, sometimes the purpose of this festival become a bit misty.

The first one I experienced was at Chiang Mai in 1980. I was teaching English in the afternoons and rode a bicycle to the school. On the way I saw three young boys peeking around a fence at me as I approached them. As I pedaled slowly past them they ambushed me with buckets of water. I must admit, jai yen was not my first thought but I didn't go back, after all, they had more water on hand. I caught a few more soakings on the way and arrived at class dripping wet. But I wasn't alone, everyone was soaked. I asked the students, "What's with the water throwing?" I got several replies and the consensus was, "Because it's hot."

The next day, I packed clothes and books into plastic bags and wore only shorts and a tee shirt. I didn't try to dodge the water and even found a Chinese shop owner who had an oil drum full of water and a couple of blocks of ice to chill it down. There, I stopped alongside and let him pour water on me. Nothing like a cold shower on a hot afternoon. Later I passed two elderly Thai men standing along the road. One held a shiny, metal bowl of water with flower blossoms floating on top, the other man held a small branch covered in leaves.

I stopped to see what they were doing and the man with the branch dipped it into the bowl of water then gently sprinkled me and said, "Chok dee," good luck. We began talking and I asked him about the meaning of the sprinkling.

"This is the way it was in the old times," he said, "Songkran was a time to forgive all of the animosity and resentments of the past year and the water symbolized the washing away of those differences. In those days everyone traveled slowly, walking or riding in a buffalo cart, and they would stop to have water sprinkled on them. It was refreshing. But now, everyone has faster transportation and the people must throw the water." To make sure that everyone is forgiven, pickup trucks loaded with drums of water and a crew of water throwers prowl the streets.

In reality, it is a playful, no-sides, every person for themselves, water fight in which the whole population takes part. If you do not want to play, stay indoors until nightfall when a temporary truce is declared. Windowless buses are a favorite target, especially when stopped for a traffic light. Be prepared to get wet just about anywhere you go. If you want to join in, arm yourself with a water gun, they are on sale everywhere, and squirt some people. If you are taking the game seriously, quit playing. This is a time to get rid of hard feelings, not get them.

Notes

Leisure Activities

Practically every sport or pastime activity that you find in any large American city is available in Bangkok. Whatever your interests are you will probably find a venue, club or organization that fulfills them and you may even discover some new ones.

The expat community has always been an element in Bangkok's social life and over the years it has established choral and musical societies, a community theater, business organizations, writers' workshops and many other common interest groups.

The sporting activities range from flying to scuba diving. Public swimming pools and tennis courts are plentiful, and many apartment buildings have them as well. Inner city parks offer rental rowboats as well as playing fields, bicycling and jogging paths. They are safe, clean and well maintained.

A short list of the sports activities for expats includes tennis, golf, bicycle trips, kayaking, trekking, traveling, sailing, scuba diving, flying. Clubs organize activities and outings and are an excellent way to cut the already reasonable costs and meet other expats.

There are scores of golf courses and numerous driving ranges in the city. The reasonable fees attract thousands of Japanese golfers each year who find it cheaper than Japan even with the airfare and hotel costs included. There is an inner-city driving range at the dead end of Soi 18 Sukhumvit where you can hire a caddy to place the ball on the tee for you. Try to find that luxury in the US.

Cultural Organizations

The international community in Bangkok is represented not only by its embassies but also by cultural institutions that present their nations' literature, theater, films and language courses to the public, often free of charge.

American Women's Club of Thailand

171-173 Soi Phromsri, Sukhumvit 49/11
Bangkok, Thailand 10110
Tel 02 381-9225
awc_Thailand@hotmail.com
http://members.tripod.com/~AWC_Th/index.htm

Alliance Francaise

29 Sathorn Tai (South) Rd.
Tel 02 213 2122

This venue presents French films, theater, and concerts in its 300 seat auditorium as well as a video club, library and lectures. A bookstore stocks French and English publications.

AUA (American University Alumni)

179 Rajadamri Rd.
Tel 02 251 1607

This association was founded by Thais who graduated from American universities for the purpose of providing English language instruction. It also presents American lecturers, guest artists, and films free of charge in the auditorium.

British Council

254 Soi 64 Phaya Thai Rd. (in Siam Square)
Tel 02 252 6136

Provides English language lessons and an excellent library. British films, dance, drama and music are presented in the auditorium.

Japanese Cultural Center

Sermmit Tower, 159 Soi 21 (Asoke) Sukhumvit Rd.
Films, lectures, exhibitions and live performances.

Goethe Institute (Thai-German Cultural Foundation)

18/1 Soi Attakarn Prasit, Sathorn Tai (South) Rd.
Tel 02 287 0942

Weekly showing of German films, film festivals and lectures are presented in the auditorium. Library includes German magazines, records, VDO tapes, and slides.

Libraries

AUA Library

179 Rajadamri Rd.
Hours: Tuesday through Friday 9 A.M. to 6 P.M.
Saturday 9 A.M. to 4:30 P.M.

Public lending library for Bangkok residents and students of AUA. Requires proof of residency (rent or utility receipt in your name), passport and a small fee. Books on general topics as well as a large section on Thai art, culture and history.

American Chamber of Commerce

7th Flr., Kian Gwan House
140 Witthayu (Wireless) Rd.
Hours: Monday through Friday 9 A.M. to 5 P.M.
Saturday 9 A.M. to 4:30 P.M.

Reference library for commercial interests. It has directories of US and Thai companies and phone books of major US cities as well as business periodicals, trade journals and US Customs reference volumes.

British Council Library

254 Phaya Thai Soi 64 (in Siam Square)
Hours: Monday through Friday 10 A.M. to 7:30 P.M.
Saturday 10 A.M. to 5 P.M.

Public lending library for Bangkok residents over 15 years of age. Requires proof of residency (rent or utility receipt in your name) passport and an annual fee. Stocks books by British authors on topics including reference, business, history, and fiction. An extensive video collection of movies, training programs and documentaries.

Neilson Hays Library

195 Surawong Rd. (near the British Club)
Hours: Tues 9:30 A.M. to 4 P.M. Wed 9:30 A.M. to 7 P.M. Thurs,
Fri, Sat 9:30 A.M. to 4 P.M. Sun 9:30 A.M. to 2 P.M.

Membership is open to all. Stocks fiction and non-fiction books. The library is supported by the members.

Bookstores

English language bookstores are plentiful in the city. They range from trendy, air conditioned shops selling new books, to open-air, market stalls selling used books. The selection is extensive and the prices are reasonable. One friend of mine conducts business through the Internet selling semi-rare books that he discovers at bookstalls.

Asia Books

Sukhumvit Rd., between Sois 15-17
World Trade Center, 3rd Flr.
Peninsula Plaza next to Regent Hotel
Landmark Hotel, Sukhumvit Rd., between Sois 4-6.
www.asiabooks.co.th

This company maintains the most complete range of English language books in Thailand. The topics it stocks include best-sellers, fiction and non-fiction, reference volumes, travel, art, business, maps, videos, and Thai language courses.

Bookazine

Siam Square opposite Tower Records
CP Tower Ground Flr, Silom Rd.
Sukhumvit Rd., between Sois 3-5

Good stock of best-sellers and recent releases.

Book Chest

Siam Square next to DK Books
Pantip Plaza, 3rd Flr., Petchburi Rd.

Computer manuals and text books.

Book Gallery

12/1 Soi 33, Sukhumvit Rd.
Good selection of international magazines.

DK Book House

Siam Square
Sukhumvit Rd. between Sois 8-10.
Wide selection of Thai and English language books and tapes.

Elite Used Books

Sukhumvit Rd., between Sois 33-35, near Villa Market.
Books in several European and Asian languages as well as English. Includes fiction, travel, reference, history and personal library collections.

Kinokuniya

World Trade Center, 6th Flr.
Emporium, Sukhumvit Rd., corner of Soi 24.
Extensive selection of English titles.

Merman Books

Silom Complex, 2nd Flr. On Silom Rd.
This shop specializes in secondhand books. The books are in easy to find categories that cover the topics of history, art, travel, military, business, and more.

PKV Book House

Sukhumvit Rd. Soi 33.
Stocks international newspapers and magazines.

The Professional Bookshop

Ploenchit Centre, Ploenchit Rd.
Good selection of books on business and computers.

Siam Society

131 Soi 21 (Asoke). Sukhumvit Rd.
www.siamsociety.org
Books on Thai history and culture.

Music and Theater

If you play an instrument, sing or act there are several organizations that welcome your participation. It's a good way to keep in practice and meet people.

Bangkok Combined Choirs

Maureen Paetkau
Tel 02 258 4234

This group performs concerts throughout the year and all singers are invited to participate. Rehearsals are held at the International Church, Sukhumvit Soi 19 on Mondays at 7 P.M. starting in mid-September.

Bangkok Music Society

MBE Asoke Suite 50, 44/1-3 Sukhumvit Soi 21.
Daphne Colwell
Tel 02 617 1880

Open to anyone who enjoys listening or performing Western, classical music. Concerts are organized with local and visiting artists and the choir performs major choral works and concert selections. Membership is gained by a simple audition and rehearsals are on Wednesdays.

Bangkok Symphony Orchestra Foundation

Khun Witaya
Tel 02 223 0871

Musicians are invited to join.

Bangkok Community Theatre (BCT)

Contact Angela Mitchell, Tel 02 258 8495
Bonnie Zellerbach, Tel 02 618 7080
Louise Truslow, Tel 02 618 4047
www.bct-th.org

A volunteer organization that presents several productions each year. Auditions are advertised in the Bangkok Post and the Nation newspapers and are open to anyone who wishes to join the group either on stage or backstage. No Experience necessary. A social night is held on the first Thursday of each month at the British Club on Silom Rd., 7:30 P.M.

Parks

Lumpini Park

Located between Wireless Rd. in the east, Rajdamri Rd. in the west, Sarasin Rd. on the north and Rama IV Rd. on the south.

This is a favored park of Bangkokians who begin arriving in the morning for *tai chi* workouts and bike riding or jogging along the park's well tended paths. There is a small lake with rowboats for rent and food carts are always nearby. A favorite beverage among the health-conscious is the snake blood cocktail from the cart at the entrance to the park. There is no threat of mugging.

Benchasiri Park

On Sukhumvit Rd. between Sois 22 and 24.

This serene, little park has a jogging track, exercise station, and volleyball courts. It is a popular setting for wedding photos.

Chatuchak Park

Next to the Weekend Market on Paholyothin Rd.

Many trees, pathways, and large expanse of lawn make the park a perfect place for a picnic or a rest after shopping at the Weekend Market.

Sports

The Amazing Bangkok Cyclist

Mr. Co Van Kessel
abc_2000@yahoo.com
> Organized bike rides throughout the city. He provides bicycle rentals and planned outings.

Bike & Travel

Tel 02 990 0900
> Specializes in organized weekend bike tours.

Phukijdee Flying Club

Bangkok Office, 15th Flr., Richmond Bldg.
75/47 Soi 26, Sukhumvit Rd.
Tel 02 262 1646
> Lessons available on weekends. Very reasonable rates. English speaking instructors.

The Capitol Club, Exercise Gym

Soi 24, Sukhumvit Rd., in President Park Complex.
Tel 02 661-1210
> Very large facility with modern, California-style machines.

The Eagle Flying Club

Ratchaburi Airport
Tel 02 541 4760
> Lessons available for very reasonable rates. From beginner to private pilot's license. English speaking instructors.

Bangkok Wanderers Golf Club

George Simpson
Tel 02 231 3663
> Play at various courses at discounted rates. Any standard of play welcome.

Phatra Yacht Club

Khun Cheerut
Tel 02 693 2842
Located at Pranburi, south of Hua Hin. Modern club with air conditioned accommodations and marina facilities. A fleet of Farr 25' keelboats available for charter.

Larry's Dive

Tel 02 663 4563
larrybkk@larrysdive.com
www.larrysdive.com.
Scuba diving instruction and equipment rental.

Sakolphan Racquet Club

219 Soi Panit Anan, Sukhumvit Soi 71
Tel 02 391 0563
Four tennis and badminton courts, swimming pool and club house.

Santisuk Tennis Court

Sukhumvit Soi 38
Tel 02 391 1830
This venue has four courts and a clubhouse.

Soi Klang Racquet Club

8 Sukhumvit Soi 49
Tel 02 391 0963
Facility has swimming pools, saunas, workout room, tennis, squash, badminton, and racquetball courts.

Notes

Income Opportunities

Bangkok is like any other large city in the world, it has income and employment opportunities. But I don't mean a "job" in the sense that there are openings in the fast-food industry, or assembling computers. These jobs belong to the Thais. There is a specific list of jobs and professions that are available only for Thai citizens. On the other hand, there are positions that are best filled by an English speaking foreigner. Teaching English is the first thing that comes to mind, but there are also opportunities for editors, writers, computer specialists and other specialized skills.

The Bangkok Post classified section always lists job opportunities for expats. From there, one friend who knew a few computer programs, scored the position of assistant editor for an English language travel magazine. She had no formal training as an editor. She was well paid and traveled extensively throughout the kingdom.

Another acquaintance replied to an ad in the Bangkok Post and was hired as the publications manager of a new cable TV station. This job included working on the Miss Universe event hosted by the station.

Though there are jobs offered to foreigners in the newspapers, these are only a few of the opportunities available. There are scores of international companies looking for English-speaking personnel but don't openly advertise for them. Instead they make a formal request to their company's human resources department, and informally let the word out to the expat community.

As a general rule, an international or Thai company that requires English speaking personnel would rather hire someone who is already in the country than take someone, sight unseen, from overseas. If you have a skill that fills a need in Thailand, your chances are good that you will find a job.

Networking is the key element to making a living in Bangkok. You've got to have friends and the expat social clubs are an excellent way to make them. For example, the Bangkok Community Theater is notified when extras are needed for movies or commercials being filmed in the kingdom. I scored two jobs this way. Teaching English is another effective way to build a network of friends who pass the word about jobs for expats.

Teaching English

Teaching English won't make you rich, but you will be able to make enough to cover your living expenses. It can also open some beneficial doors.

I once lived on Ko Samui where I rented a furnished house near the beach. The rent was US $100 a month and daily expenses averaged around $5. About $250-300 a month not counting the money it took to make the visa runs to Malaysia. When I rented the house I reported my address with the Immigration Office as a matter of formality and while there, one of the officers asked if I would give him English lessons. I agreed and after several lessons he told me of a bungalow resort that wanted someone to teach English to the staff. Through word of mouth, that one contact led to more accounts and I was able to start saving some money. At some of the resorts I traded lessons for meals or lodging, others paid in cash. Not a lot of money, but certainly enough to make it worth my while, and make a lot of friends.

A British friend of mine specialized in resort hotels where he proposed an English course for the staff. He contracted for a cash payment plus room and board.

You don't need to speak the Thai language in order to teach English since all classes are conducted in English. What's more, in many cases you don't need teaching or college credentials, although a certified applicant will be chosen over one who isn't. The pay is also better for the person who has completed a course for teaching English as a foreign language (TEFL). English teachers need not be native speakers but Americans, Canadians, New Zealanders, Australians and British citizens are preferred.

The schools provide the course books and teaching aids and test the students for their level of understanding. The classes are men and women of various ages, except for one class of monks I had where women weren't allowed into the room.

The students are often very proficient in reading and writing English but are unpracticed in hearing the sounds of the language and understanding its idioms. Because vowels are the most important sounds in the Thai language, consonants used in English -- especially when they occur at the ends of words -- are the trouble spots for Thai students. Clear enunciation of words is essential, as is the elimination of non-essential phrases such as " you know", "and um," "but uh" and other speech fillers. Your students will try to copy everything you say and assume that it is correct. I met one student who had copied her American boyfriend's speech habits and used the phrase "you know" before, after, and in the middle of practically every statement.

The students are polite and unruly classrooms are rare, they come to learn. As a teacher you will be respected for openers, but it is possible to lose that status by not preparing the lesson, bad manners, or by showing a lack of decorum for your students by sloppy dressing or grooming.

Class preparation means not only preparing the lesson as it is presented in the teaching materials but also including activities that are stimulating, challenging and even fun. Role playing is a good way to begin a class. Students are often late and it's a good idea to have a short exercise while waiting for all of them to show up. One scenario that students enjoy is shopping. I'll give each student a few bills of play money and then assume the role of a vendor using fried bananas or some other Thai snack as my product. Then I invite each student to make a purchase from me, and bargain. Try to make your classes entertaining as well as instructive and you and the students will enjoy them.

Your deportment and appearance will be "on stage" any time you are in view of your students or staff at the school. You can lose a lot of "face" without even knowing it by getting angry, wearing a scowl, or gossiping about the students or school. As a teacher, whether you are qualified or not, the students automatically give you the respect due to a professional. They will address you as *kru*, teacher, and you will be expected to dress and behave in a respectful manner.

As a teacher, you will have many opportunities to enlarge your social life and make friends within the Thai community. Your students will often invite you out for a meal or to visit their homes.

The rate of pay for teachers runs from $5 to $15 an hour depending on your qualifications and the school's pay policy. Many of the schools offer work permits for English teachers.

There are companies that provide teachers for home study. This is generally limited to the Japanese and Korean expat communities, usually executives' families of companies operating in Thailand. Their children attend an international school where English is the language and the kids must get up to speed quickly in order to attend. One friend of mine taught Japanese kids from Sesame Street books for $15 an hour.

Your first job might be only a couple of classes a week for openers. But the schools always have a huge turnover of teachers and if you suit up and show up you will be called on to fill in when other teachers have to miss classes or quit in the middle of a course. In addition, you may well work for two or more schools at the same time.

The best way to look for a teaching job is to present yourself in person. Make a one-page resume with a passport photo attached. List only the activities and certificates that are relevant. Then present copies to the schools you are interested in working for. You may be hired on an hourly basis or offered a contract. Either way, the school is responsible for processing your work permit application, if you are qualified, or keeping you out of harm's way if you are not.

It's an open secret that many English teachers working in Thailand are doing so without a permit. The schools are rarely raided, however, and the issue only comes up with the police or Immigration authorities when you get into trouble in other ways and you are required to show how you have supported yourself while living in the kingdom.

There are other regulations to meet before you are a legal teacher in Thailand, a non-immigrant visa, a Teacher's Card and a Tax Card. Inquire when you apply at a school.

While universities and government organizations require potential employees to have a degree, if you have some college training in almost any discipline you'll be able to get a job at a language center if you pass the written literacy test that is given by the school.

Websites for teaching jobs

www.tefl.net

If you have TEFL (Teaching English as a Foreign Language) qualifications, the range of job opportunities available to you broadens and the pay is better. Visit this site for more information.

www.ajarn.com

The best source of information on teaching in Thailand is Ajarn.com. This site includes everything you need to know about teaching English in Thailand. It lists local jobs, tips of the trade, which jobs to go for and which ones to avoid.

Dave's ESL Cafe www.daveseslcafe.com

Escape Artist   www.escapeartist.com

English Language Schools

There are dozens of language schools in the city. Their pay rates and requirements vary from one to the other, but the best paying require certified teachers.

Many of the schools have branches in other parts of the kingdom and you can secure a job in the provinces if you wish.

Besides teaching in the classroom there are opportunities for private tutoring of business or professional groups.

AUA

179 Rajadamri Rd.
Tel 02 252 8170
www.auathailand.com

This school is very popular with students and teachers. Pay is around 25,000 baht per month. Check the website for details.

British American

Lad Prao Rd., Soi 58-60
Tel 02 934 9181
British_American2000@hotmail.com

A large organization with many branches. Pay is around 25,000 baht per month.

Bell Language Schools

204/1 Ranong 1 Rd,
Samsen, Dusit, Bangkok 10300
Tel 02 241 0356   Fax 02 668 2124
gbradd@loxinfo.co.th
www.bell-centres.com/locations/Thailand.html
> This school offers salaries of 30,000 baht and has branches in several locations. Check the website for details.

Henley Communications Ltd.

Tel 02 937 0827
> An agency based in the Chatuchak area and pays over 500 baht an hour, usually for business language classes.

Elite Training Institute

Kongboonma Bldg., 2nd Flr.
699 Silom Rd., Bangkok 10500
Tel 02 635   Fax 02 237 1997
elite@eliteinstitute.com
www.eliteinstitute.com
> An agency as well as a language school. It contracts teachers for around 30,000 baht. Check the website for details.

Fun Language International

Lee House, 4th Floor
275 Soi 55 (Thonglor) 13, Bangkok 10110
Tel 02 712 7744   Fax 02 712 7733
engisfun@loxinfo.co.th
www.geocities.com/TheTropics/Harbor/8822
> Specializes in teaching English as a foreign language to children aged 3 and up using Fun Language Method. Check the website for details.

ECC (Thailand)

430/17-24 Chula Soi 64
Siam Square, Bangkok
Tel 02 235 3311
www.eccThai.com/eccThai

This is the largest private language school in Thailand and is always recruiting teachers. Acceptance requires some qualifications to be met with. Check out the website for full details.

Siam Computer & Language Institute

471/19 Ratchawithi Rd.
Tel 02 247 2345

This institute has 35 schools in Greater Bangkok. It is always hiring teachers.

Writing and Editing

There are also opportunities for editors, story writers, ad copy writers, and fast, accurate copy typists since practically every English language publishing company needs a native English-speaking person on the staff at one time or another. The openings include full-time, part time, or contract positions.

I once contracted to work on a series of directories that were being produced for the foreign Chambers of Commerce in Bangkok. It was straight copy typing and I was paid according to the amount of work I produced. Although speed-typing a catalog of names and phone numbers is not my favorite work, it wasn't terminal and only lasted a month. But while I was there, I met other expats, free-lancers like myself, and we exchanged information on work opportunities. One fellow turned me on to a copy writing job with an ad agency where I received several assignments.

I once answered an ad in the Bangkok Post and was contracted to rewrite a travel guide to South Thailand. Another time, a friend turned me on to a English language business magazine that was looking for a staff writer.

Exporting

If you like the marketing game then exporting Thai products, especially handicrafts, may be for you. For a few years I exported paintings, lacquer ware, hand painted umbrellas and fans to the US where I had a partner who sold them at Saturday markets. The process was simple. Buy the products, pack them into a one cubic meter box and consign them to a shipper who took care of the paperwork and shipping arrangements. There is no duty on Thai handicrafts into the US and the shipping was straightforward. I kept the money value of the shipment at a level that qualified for a "non-commercial, samples" status.

Shipping to the US by sea takes from two to three months. Sea freight charges are based on a minimum charge for one cubic meter, and depend on the customs classification of the shipment. For example, one cubic meter held 300, 20" paper umbrellas. If I classified them as umbrellas the cost was $120. If I listed the shipment as "bamboo ware" the cost was $60. This was the difference a few years ago so the figures are not valid today.

Air freight is economical for light weight shipments and small objects. The air freight calculations are based on a minimum, weight/size ratio. That means you buy x amount of space and in that space you can put x amount of weight. Quite often, when shipping light weight objects, the space dimensions are the important factor, so you can add to the shipment until you have reached your space/weight limits. This spreads the cost of the shipment around.

If you are new to the game, make yourself aware of the export and import laws of the countries involved. For example, because of US import quotas you can export silk but not cotton to the US, and Thai export regulations prohibit export of Buddha images without special permission. Libraries and bookstores stock numerous books on importing and exporting.

Asia Books

Sukhumvit Rd., between Sois 15-17
www.asiabooks.co.th

This branch has a large selection of current business books in English.

The American Chamber of Commerce Thailand

Kian Gwan Bldg. 2, 18th Floor
140/1 Wireless Rd.
Lumpini, Bangkok 10330
Tel. 02 2251 9266   Fax. 02 2651 4472
info@amchamThailand.com
www.amchamThailand.org

> Reference library for commercial interests. Directories and phone books of US and Thai companies and cities as well as business periodicals.

Websites

www.businessinThailandmag.com/msindex.html
www.doingbusinessinThai.com
www.amchamThailand.org

Going Into Business

Thailand and America have joined in a Treaty of Amity and Economic Relations which is very favorable to Americans who start businesses in the kingdom. Details of the treaty can be found at the website www.thailawforum.com/database1/amity.html

You will probably come up with ideas and methods for establishing a business in the kingdom and although you will be required to jump through some bureaucratic hoops, the process in most cases is not all that difficult but it will take time. A lot depends on the nature of the business, manufacturing, service, or sales.

An expat I knew started an office cleaning business in Bangkok. He managed it very efficiently and ended up selling it for a handsome amount of money and was then hired on to manage the company. A couple of other acquaintances, a Canadian and an American, opened a construction consulting business. One fellow, a recording technician from New York, arrived in the city a few years ago armed only with his skill. He started a recording business from scratch that is now very successful. When he arrived he looked for opportunity, not a job. He studied Thai, got into the music scene where he made friends with musicians and recording producers then sold his idea to a Thai partner.

Do You Have a Money Making Skill or Hobby?

A teacher I worked with at the Chiang Mai AUA was running low on money and put her Canon camera up for sale on the bulletin board there. She wasn't a professional photographer and figured that she could get by with a cheaper camera. A few days later she met with an interested buyer, a South African woman who was an owner of a company that made gold plated, orchid jewelry. "I took along some photos I had taken with the camera," my friend said, "and the buyer was so impressed with them that she asked me to take the pictures for a catalog the company was producing. The buyer told me she was only interested in the camera for this reason and that she would still have to learn to take pictures."

"I had never made a photography contract before, so I went to the AUA library and found just what I needed, a book on how to be a professional photographer. I did a quick study on writing photo contracts and pricing the work, then simply copied the sample contract from the book, with all the 'if' and 'whereas' clauses and sold each photo for $20. They bought two rolls of film -- and accepted all 72 slides!"

Another young woman, a trained secretary, got a contract transcribing English language tape recordings to disk. Fast, accurate typing and editing in English is always a marketable skill.

Another entrepreneur published The Trading Post, an English language shoppers' newspaper. He sold ads to restaurants, supermarkets, tailors, sports bars as well as classified ads from expats. It was distributed throughout the city in grocery stores, beauty shops, restaurants and places that expatriates frequented.

An American I know began a business supplying custom-made, inlaid picture frames to buyers in the US and Europe. Another expat started a peanut butter manufacturing company. Still another initiated an all-inclusive golf tour of the country which is marketed in the US, Japan and Europe.

Thailand is a model of free enterprise where entrepreneurs can formulate ideas, test them out, and put them into full operation within a reasonable amount of time and the government regulations for Americans in business are more encouraging than negative. Since regulations are subject to change, it is best to consult with a business center for assistance.

Business Centers

Check out the business centers in the major hotels. Most of them have an English language reference library and Thai commercial phone books in English. They offer translation, typing and secretarial services as well as fax, Email and phone.

Landmark Hotel

138 Sukhumvit Rd., between Sois 6-8
www.landmarkbangkok.com

Amari Boulevard Hotel

2 Soi 5 Sukhumvit Rd., Bangkok 10110
boulevard@mozart.inet.co.th

JPB Business Services

Times Square Bldg., Suite 211
Sukhumvit Rd., between Sois 12 and 14
Tel 02 653 3636   Fax 02 653 3635
Open from 10 A.M. to 10 P.M.

Provides Internet service, international phone calls, printing, scanning, photocopying as well as assistance on work permits, visas, business setup, income taxes, and translation services.

178

International Schools

For English-speaking expats with children or those who wish to further their education, Bangkok has a large selection of schools and courses ranging from preschool to postgraduate level.

Points to consider when choosing a school,

√ How far is the school from your home?

√ Does the school provide transportation?

√ What are the student to staff ratios?

√ What are the qualifications of the staff?

√ What is the class size?

√ Is the curriculum compatible with your home country?

√ What are the examination results of the school?

√ Are remedial and extracurricular programs offered?

Fees

Fees often include registration, tuition, transportation, school lunches and extra curricular activities. Ask the school to list what is included in their fee structure.

Format

International schools follow the United Kingdom or the North American educational model and are staffed with accredited instructors from their respective countries. They offer extra-curricular activities that include sports, music, and foreign language instruction.

The universities present many courses for students who are working towards a degree as well as post graduate work and the cost is quite affordable.

The listings provided here give only a sketch of the schools' offerings and amenities, check out the websites for more details.

Preschool and Kindergarten

Bangkok Patana School (BPS)

2/38 Sukhumvit Soi 105 (Lasalle), Bangkok 10260
Tel 02 398 0200
registrar@patana.ac.th
www.patana.ac.th
Offers a preschool program from 2 years of age.

International Pre School Center

313 Soi 31 Sukhumvit Rd., Bangkok 10110
Tel 02258 8105
ipsc2@ksc.th.com
www.ipcThai.com
In business for 20 years accepts children from 1.5 years.
Hours 8:30 A.M. to noon.

KiddyKare International Kindergarten

16 Sukhumvit Soi 24, Bangkok 10110
Tel 02 661 1333
infoatkiddykare.com
www.kiddykare.com
Accepts children from 1.5 to 6 years old. Hours 8:30 A.M. to 2 P.M. After-care available until 6 P.M.

The American School of Bangkok (ASB)

3 Sukhumvit Soi 49, Bangkok 10110
Tel 02 258 7829
diselem@samart.co.th
www.dis.ac.th
For children from 2 years old.

Topsy Turvy International School

36 Sukhumvit Soi 4, Bangkok 10110
Tel 02 656 9961
info@topsy-turvy.com
www.topsy-turvy.com
For children from 1 to 6 years old. Hours from   8:30 A.M. to
2 P.M.

Twinkle Star Nursery School

81 Sukhumvit Soi 61, Bangkok 10110
Tel 02 381 3094
In business for 20 years accepts children from 2 to 6 years.
Curriculum includes reading, art, music, cooking and
exercises.

Primary and Secondary Schools

International School Bangkok

39/7 Soi Nichada Thani, Samakee Rd.
Pakkret, Nonthaburi 11120
Tel 02 583 5401
jamess@isb.ac.th
www.isb.ac.th
This is a college preparatory school with most of the teachers
and about 33% of the students from the USA. It accepts
students from 5 to 18 years of age and uses the North
American curriculum. Check the Website for details.

Ruamrudee International School (RIS)

42 Moo 4, Soi 184
Ramkamhaeng, Rd., Minburi, Bangkok 10510
Tel 02 518 0320
director@rism.ac.th
> This school includes kindergarten to the 12th grade with the high school curriculum focused towards college preparation. Excellent reputation and accreditation. Check the Website for details.

The American School of Bangkok (ASB)

3 Sukhumvit Soi 49, Bangkok 10110
Tel 02 258 7829
diselem@samart.co.th
www.dis.ac.th
> For grades kindergarten through 12. It has boarding facilities. Check Website for details.

The New International School of Thailand

36 Sukhumvit Soi 15, Bangkok 10110
Tel 02 253 3751
nist@nist.ac.th
www.nist.ac.th
> This school is related to the United Nations and the curriculum is based on the UN philosophy. It is fully accredited and accepts students from all nationalities. Check Website for details.

University Education

Attending university in Thailand will give you some rewarding experience that can put you ahead of others in the job market, and it also provides you with the network required to find the best teaching jobs.

There are several universities in Thailand that offer international programs, both undergraduate and graduate level, that are taught exclusively in English, and they are reasonably priced.

At Bangkok University the cost of a master's degree program, including tuition, fees and books, is around $5,000 and takes approximately two years to complete. Also in Bangkok, Assumption University and Chulalongkorn University offer an MA program in Thai Studies as well as degrees from the highly respected Sasin Graduate School of Business Administration

Some of the universities in Thailand are recognized throughout Asia and maintain exchange programs with universities throughout the world.

Many of the professors have doctoral degrees from universities in the United States or Europe and have held positions in the world of commerce, government, and academia.

Veterans of the US Armed Forces can use their GI Bill to study in Thailand at universities approved by the Department of Veteran's Affairs. A friend of mine says his GI Bill payments cover tuition, books, university fees as well as his rent.

Application to attend a university can be made either before or after you arrive in the kingdom. To receive a student visa, you must first be approved by the Ministry of Education. The college submits your application for approval and when you have been accepted the college forwards copies of the approval documents to you and the Thai Consulate for processing the student visa. With this visa you can work part time, without a work permit.

Asian Institute of Technology
www.ait.ac.th

Assumption University
www.au.ac.th

Bangkok University International College
www.bu.ac.th

Chulalongkorn University
www.chula.ac.th

Kasem Bundit University
www.kbu.ac.th

King Mongkut's University
www.kmitnb.ac.th

Mahidol University
www.mahidol.ac.th

Ramkhamhaeng University
www.ru.ac.th

Notes

Internet Addresses

BANKS
Bangkok Bank   www.bbl.co.th

Siam Commercial Bank   www.scb.co.th

BUSINESS CONTACTS AND WEB MAGAZINES
US Chamber of Commerce   www.amchamthailand.org

Business In Thailand   www.biz-in-thailand.com

www.businessinThailandmag.com

www.doingbusinessinThai.com

CONSULATES
US Consulate in Bangkok   acsbkk@state.gov

US Passport   www.travel.state.gov/passport_services.html

Thai Consulate   www.thai-la.net

EDUCATION
PRE SCHOOLS
Bangkok Patana   www.patana.ac.th

International School   www.ipcthai.com

KiddyKare   www.kiddykare.com

American School   www.dis.ac.th

Topsy Turvy   www.topsy-turvy.com

PRIMARY/SECONDARY SCHOOLS
International Bangkok   www.isb.ac.th

International Thailand   www.nist.ac.th

Bangkok Patana   www.patana.ac.th

UNIVERSITIES
Bangkok University   www.bu.ac.th

Assumption University   www.au.ac.th

Chulalongkorn University   www.chula.ac.th

GENERAL INFORMATION

Asia Books	www.asiabooks.com
Bangkok Cuisine	www.bangkokcuisine.com
Bangkok Post	www.bangkokpost.com
DHL Shipping	www.dhl.com
FedEx Shipping	www.fedex.com
Tops Marketplace	www.tops.co.th
Western Union	www.westernunion.com

HEALTH

Blue Cross (BUPA)	www.bupathailand.com
Bangkok Gen. Hospital	www.bgh.co.th
Bangkok Nursing Home	www.bangkoknursinghome.com
Bumrungrad Hospital	www.bumrungrad.com
St Louis Hospital	www.saintlouis.or.th
Samitivej Hospital	www.samitivej.co.th

HOTELS AND APARTMENTS

Ambassador Hotel	www.amtel.co.th
Nana Hotel	www.nanahotel.co.th
Budget Hotel List	www.thaihotel.com
Hotels in Bangkok	www.hotelsinbangkok.com
Bangkok Post	www.bangkokpost.net/classifieds
Boss Tower	www.bosstower.com
Maple House	www.maplehouseapartment.com
Bangkok-homes	www.bangkok-homes.com
Sky Place	www.sccskyplace.com
Apartment Bangkok	www.apartmentbangkok.com
Chantra Court	www.chatra99.com
Rentals in Thailand	www.rentalsinthailand.com

Starry Place	www.starryplace.com
The Residence	www.residence-hotel.com
Grand Hi-Tech	www.grandhitechtower.com
InterCourt Apt.	www.intercourtapartment.com

INTERNET SERVICE PROVIDERS

Loxley Information	www.loxinfo.co.th
Samart Cybernet	www.samart.co.th
Internet Thailand	www.inet.co.th

TEACHING

English Teachers	www.ajarn.com
AUA Language	www.auathailand.com
Bell Schools	www.bell-centres.com
Elite Training	www.eliteinstitute.com
ECC (Thailand)	www.eccthai.com/eccthai
Fun Language	www.geocities.com
TEFL Site	www.tefl.net
English Teachers	www.ajarn.com
Dave's ESL Cafe	www.daveseslcafe.com
Escape Artist	www.escapeartist.com

TRANSPORTATION

City Map	www.asiaaccess.net.th/citymap/html
Songserm Travel	www.asiatravel.com/songserm
Skytrain	www.bts.co.th
Train Reservations	www.srt.motc.go.th/httpEng
Thailand Airports	www.airportthai.or.th

188

Smuggling activities across the Thai-Malaysia border are open secrets, and the traffic is two-way. There was even a movie made about a young boy and his family of smugglers who lived at Padang Besar, the border crossing between Thailand and Malaysia. But the movie did not feature the swift, International Express train because years ago the Express only ran two days a week and train travel to Malaysia on the other days was made in two stages. The first ended at Had Yai, a city near the Thai-Malaysian border. From there it was a self-propelled railcar train to Butterworth called the Smuggler's Slowcoach. A train I discovered when I arrived in Had Yai on my first visa run to Penang.

"I'd like a second-class ticket to Butterworth, please."

The agent behind the counter at the Hat Yai train station shook his head and said, "Today's train is third-class. The International Express comes tomorrow, maybe it will have second-class."

"I'll take third-class, then," I said indifferently, although I dreaded the thought of a hard-seat train ride on a hot April afternoon.

I had been living in Bangkok for three months and my visa was nearly expired, so I had to hit the Visa Trail for the Thai Consulate in Penang, Malaysia, 500 miles south of Bangkok. It was 1981, and the International Express — one, fast, comfortable, air-conditioned train all the way — made the trip on two days a week but I was unable to book a seat and had to do the "Visa Two-Step" instead. From Bangkok, I rode an overnight train, sleeping in a berth surrounded by all the creature comforts, to Had Yai. There, I embarked on the bare-bones Smuggler's Slowcoach to Butterworth Station, near Penang.

I expected to see a regular train with the locomotive and coaches, instead, it consisted of four, self-propelled cars coupled together. But unlike new railcars made entirely of metal with automatic doors in the middle, this train's interior was finished with wood and the boarding steps were located at the ends of the cars, showing them to be at least 20 years old. But the faded colors coated with a patina of dust and grime, the flaking, silver paint on the roof sutured with cataracts of black caulking tracing where countless leaks had been patched, and the well worn interior made it look more like 50. The windows and doors were wide open and the dust and heat wafted freely through this border crosser as it roasted patiently in the afternoon sun.

Inside, people struggled to find room for their bodies and baggage. The seats were all taken when I boarded so I squeezed in along the side, sat on my pack and observed my fellow passengers. Two young European couples stood across from me, nervously guarding backpacks the size of Volkswagens. Like tourists everywhere, they were trying to "get away from it all" while bringing most of "it" with them. The rest of the passengers were Southern Thais and Malays; and colorful batik sarongs mixed with the earth tones of Muslim shawls and the dark blue of Thai farmer's clothing.

Voices competed for attention as the passengers shouted greetings and gossiped with each other, joyous as a bunch of compulsive shoppers returning from a binge at the mall. One enterprising Thai woman, obviously a regular passenger, sat on the small, baggage shelf at the end of the car and set up a refreshment stand, selling cigarettes at two for one baht, chewing gum by the stick, candy by the piece, and warm soft drinks. She did a brisk business but folded her operation when the train left the station, by then the car was so full that there wasn't room for the luxury of a snack bar.

These border-crossers were serious shoppers. Large sacks of rice lay in the aisle. Stacks of packaged foods were everywhere and the overhead luggage racks were stuffed with commercial quantities of toiletries. I thought to myself, "a case of toothpaste? A gross of disposable razors? A dozen-pack of talcum powder? This stuff can't be contraband. The first test came five minutes from the station when the train stopped to pick up the Thai Customs officers. It got underway again as they began their inspection.

A crisply uniformed, stone faced officer entered the car and questioned the passengers about the contents of the bags and boxes. He stopped occasionally to write on a clipboard he carried, then casually pointed his pen at a sack of rice and said, "Whose is this?"

A middle-aged Thai woman timidly raised her hand. When the officer began questioning her she appeared confused and embarrassed, then said that although it was "illegal" rice, it was meant for her family, not for resale as the officers might think. She started out with low-voiced entreaties and built to a crescendo bursting with tearful pleadings. He listened to her for a couple of minutes but remained impassive. Finally, amid her yelps of protest, he put his clipboard down and dragged the bag to the door. A few minutes later, the train stopped and the inspectors departed taking the confiscated goods to waiting trucks. As the train pulled away, the woman's sobs changed abruptly to giggles as she and an accomplice dragged another bag of rice out from under a seat and stowed it under removable floorboards. The other passengers also swung into action and began stowing their cargoes into well established hiding places.

Looking down the aisle I could see the people in the other cars busily doing the same thing. Cartons were opened and their contents were stashed into every available enclosure, niche, recess, nook and compartment in the train. A young man carrying boxes of cookies, candies, disposable razors and clutching a screwdriver went into the water closet. He emerged a few minutes later, twirling the screwdriver. I glanced into the water closet — no smuggled goods in there. Then he pulled the floorboards up and loaded sacks of rice into the empty battery compartments. Wooden panels were removed and goods packed inside and panels replaced. Even the thin seat backs provided concealments. This high-speed activity resembled a stage play with the curtain down and the actors urgently setting the scene for the next act — The Border.

Since it never exceeded 15 m.p.h., the Smuggler's Slowcoach hardly needed to brake as it approached the Padang Besar border station. Stealth was obviously part of its deception. Here the train waited for an hour while Immigration officials scrutinized passports and Malaysian Customs men inspected the train. There were some minor disputes over the tax status of some of the "baggage" but this troupe of grey market entrepreneurs were quick to ad-lib the situations and played a skillful game of Win Some, Lose Some. The Slowcoach finally entered Malaysia and attained its highball speed of 15 m.p.h..

In contrast to the lethargy of the train, the smugglers were busier than a team of one-armed paperhangers. They retrieved their illicit cargo from its hiding places and began filling cardboard boxes with assortments of merchandise. The "Chief" of the operation was a husky Thai-Malay-Chinese woman in her thirties who went through the cars accompanied by her aide-de-camp, Mr. Screwdriver. She checked the contents of each box with a list she carried and sent Mr. Screwdriver to get more tubes of toothpaste, rice crispy cakes or whatever else was needed to fill the order. The packing frenzy finally ebbed and the cartons were placed near the doors at the end of the cars. The smuggling crew, mostly teen aged boys and girls, dozed wherever they could find room. Some played cards on the baggage shelf. Others gathered around the doors to smoke and flirt. As we click-clacked leisurely into Malaysia, amber sunlight slanted through the windows and basted everyone with perspiration while illuminating the millions of homeless dust motes that floated through the train.

The "Chief" didn't rest but strolled through the train inspecting the shipment preparations. Then she pushed her way to an open window and leaned out, her red head scarf fluttering in the wind, her narrowed eyes searching the landscape ahead. Suddenly, she ducked inside and gave an order. The card players abandoned their game and moved quickly to their action stations forming delivery teams. Mr. Screwdriver stood on the boarding steps. Behind him stood two boys and a girl each holding sealed cartons. Still leaning out the window, The "Chief" gave another command and Mr. Screwdriver lobbed a carton into the tall grass beside the tracks. A man popped up above the grass, recovered the box and scooted off on a motorbike. Another command; another box launched into the grass cushion; another man and motorcycle. Another. And another. All the passengers watched the operation and cheered loudly at each delivery. The "Chief" basked in the attention and assumed the serious demeanor of a rebel Cargo Mistress dropping supplies to a village besieged by unfair tariffs.

Afterwards, the smugglers reveled in their popularity while the passengers were equally excited by this interesting diversion and the mood turned festive. Everyone shared tobacco, jokes and the occasional bottle of whiskey that made the rounds. At one point, an old man hopped up on one leg and dramatically related how he lost the other one in a war. Then, as if to show that it didn't matter, he broke into a song-and-dance routine, a sprightly one-step with a crutch while his equally tipsy friend accompanied him with a harmonica. It was a class act and the onlookers applauded and joked with him as he cadged cigarettes from the crowd.

There were several more drops that afternoon, but each time there were fewer people to celebrate with as passengers got off and no new ones got on. At dusk, the train crept through the outskirts of Butterworth so slowly that people jumped off as we neared their homes. The dozen or so farang "visa runners" had the train all to themselves as it pulled into the station. No smugglers here.

Although the Smugglers' Slowcoach retired a few years ago smuggling continues on the International Express, though much less visible and without a hint of the excitement of the past.

Sea Trekking in Thailand

Hurled by wind and wave, the catamaran Sea Traders charged southwards along the western shore of the Gulf of Thailand. Five miles away, the port of Chumpon hid under a thick monsoon haze, its location validated by a score of shrimp trawlers aiming at its entrance, their dry-stack, diesel engines bellowing as they raced towards shelter, hoping to beat the approaching storm.

It was late afternoon and the north wind that greeted the day in Prachuap Khiri Khan 100 miles north as little more than a zephyr, now blew at 25 knots. In this playful mood, it rolled legions of waves across the Gulf, then pumped them up to eight-feet in the shoal water off of Chumpon.

But while the trawlers buried their noses and rolled on their ears, our 35' Polynesian catamaran thrived on the conditions and flew over the sea like a twin-hulled windsurfer. For the crew of _Sea Traders_, it was our reason for being there.

A couple of months before, Bianca, Peter and I worked as English teachers in landlocked Northern Thailand. Then, on a visa-run holiday I discovered a 35' catamaran for sale in Pattaya, a seaside resort on the eastern shore of the Gulf of Thailand. It had been slightly damaged when it drifted off its anchorage during a storm and collided with the seawall. The owner, a Thai windsurfing champion, didn't want it anymore and offered it to me for $2000. I called Peter and Bianca on the phone and we agreed to buy the boat.

We quit our jobs and moved to Pattaya where we spent the next six weeks preparing for a sea trek in the Gulf of Thailand. While Bianca and I had previously worked as cruising yacht sailors, Peter had never sailed before but was a quick learner. He spoke excellent Thai and while on his "missions from the boat" he collected a covey of girlfriends. Bianca and I nicknamed him, "Sailbad the Sinner."

When the repairs were completed, we christened the boat Sea Traders and departed Pattaya on the evening tide. The course was due west across the gulf on the first leg of the voyage to Ko Samui, a resort island in Southern Thailand.

We gained our sea legs on a smooth crossing and the next evening anchored along the western shore between the towns of Hua Hin and Prachuap Khiri Khan. The next day we sailed into the harbor at Prachuap Khiri Khan and anchored among the shrimp trawlers. A little while later a Thai Customs boat pulled alongside and two officers came on board to inspect our boat. This port gets a lot of smuggler traffic since it is only a few miles from the border with Burma. When they finished we gathered on the deck for a cup of coffee. The both spoke English and we chatted for a few minutes before one of them said, "Where's the motor?" Sailbad reached down to the deck and picked up an oar, "Here's one of them," The officers had a hard time believing that we would not have a motor for such a large boat. The fact was that the "Armstrong Outboards," two oars, could easily move the boat in a calm sea, and who needs a motor when there's wind?

Sea Traders departed Prachuap Khiri Khan the next morning with just enough breeze to clear the harbor. We headed south, ghosting along the coast five miles offshore. By noon the wind had increased and was pushing the boat along at 8 knots. Two hours later we were doing 12 to 15 knots with the wind and waves at our back. Cloud masses rising in the east told us that act two of a three-act storm coming. We had to find shelter, quickly.

Chumpon Harbor was out. We could have made it there easily. Just follow the trawlers, but once inside the harbor it's every captain for himself and collisions are not uncommon. We learned that from a near miss the night before in Prachuap Khiri Khan when we had to fend off a trawler that was dragging its anchor through the anchorage. About seven miles south of Chumpon is Ao Sawi, a sheltered bay with a small cove nestled in the northeast corner that offered a protected anchorage. We set our new course and, sailsurfing at 15 knots, showed our rooster tails to the fishing fleet as Sea Traders threaded her way through the maze of offshore islands to the entrance of Ao Sawi. There we skidded the boat through a ninety-degree turn and into the calm waters of the bay. The cove was easy to find and had only three, anchored trawlers,

The scene was vintage Thailand. Craggy, jungle covered ridges formed a majestic windbreak where birds of prey circled on the thermals. The narrow coastal plain was a forest of coco-palms punctuated by a thin column of white smoke. A few canoes lay beached on the thin crescent of beige sand. We anchored close to shore, completely protected from the storm in the Gulf.

"We might be here for a few days," I said, "I wonder what the people are like?"

"We'll know in a few minutes." Bianca said, "here come a couple of them now."

A dugout canoe glided towards us powered by twin "Armstrong" outboards — an old man and a young boy paddling in unison. As they came alongside, the old man held up a fish and said something in Thai.

"He wants to know if we want to buy some fish," Sailbad said.

"Maybe he just want's to check us out. It's his neighborhood," I said, "Ask him to come aboard."

I tied off the canoe while Sailbad helped them up on deck. Bianca served them a glass of water — the customary Thai icebreaker — and with Sailbad as interpreter, we had a fairly understood conversation with them. The old man was the boy's grandfather, so we called him Phuu. He wore faded, blue shorts and a stained, tee shirt with a Singha Beer logo. His craggy face with its quick, toothless smile and mahogany colored skin told of a lifetime on the water as did his thin build and ropy muscles — no overweight, out of shape people in his game. He explained that he collected bird's nests, the ones used to make Chinese soup, but couldn't get to his island base because of the weather, so he went fishing instead.

He was very interested in our boat so we showed him around. At one point he asked, "Where is the engine?" When I said we didn't have one I couldn't tell if he was impressed or thought us fools. Either way, when I invited him to go sailing the next day, his smile told me that he hoped I would ask.

Phuu and the boy came out to the boat the next morning and we set sail to investigate Sawi Bay. Although the wind still churned up the Gulf, here the water was flat, with just enough breeze wafting over the hills to push us along at five knots. Phuu was as eager to learn about sailing as we sere to discover the secrets of Sawi and it wasn't long before he was steering the catamaran. He called Sea Traders an "old man's boat" because it was so stable and easy to move around on. But he upgraded his definition when a rainsquall hit us and the boat quickly accelerated across the calm water.

We explored the Sawi coast, venturing into places we would not have dared without Phuu's guidance. That evening, we went to Phuu's house in the coconut grove and took freshwater baths from the klong jars, ate rice curry and passed the hours sharing sea-stories, tobacco, and friendship around the glow of a hissing pressure lantern. Phuu predicted clearing weather for the next day and added that he was going to his island in the morning. Would we care to go with him? You bet.

The wind in the Gulf died down overnight and the next morning we loaded Phuu's supplies on board and, towing his canoe, set off for the bird nest island, a small lump on the horizon five miles to the southeast. As we approached, the island's steep sides appeared impenetrable but Phuu guided us to a narrow passage between rocky outcrops that led into a protected lagoon where we beached the boat and tied it to palm tree.

Phuu, who had been studying the island intently as we approached, now became a man of action. He unrolled a blanket that was stowed in his canoe and picked up a single barrel shotgun.

I asked, "What's that for? Hunting birds in the cave?" I tried to make a joke.

Sailbad translated the question and Phuu replied, "<u>Kamoy</u>."

"Thieves," Sailbad said, "He wants us to go with him."

With the price of bird's nests at several hundred dollars a pound, poachers were a constant threat.

We followed Phuu into the jungle and began ascending a ridge, at the top we rested under a small lean-to. This was Phuu's lookout post and its location gave a panoramic view of the island and especially the bird nest grottoes on the north end. He scanned the view thoroughly and then led us down the trail to the caves near the shore where the birds roosted. In one cavern he demonstrated his agility by clambering up rickety, bamboo scaffolding to inspect his unusual treasure. Everything seemed in order so he led us back to the boat where we unloaded his canoe and supplies.

We fixed lunch at Phuu's island house, actually a palm frond and split-bamboo bungalow furnished with a sleeping platform and a low table. He invited us to stay as long as we wished and we did. After three lazy days of exploring the ridge and snorkeling in the lagoon, it was time to leave. Phuu stood on the shore and waied as we sailed out of the lagoon.

I looked at the simple hut, nestled in its idyllic jungle setting, secluded from the world, yet charged with the possibility of adventure. I know people who would pay for a few days of life like this. In fact, thousands of vacationers each year attempt to do so on the island of Ko Samui, our next landfall.

Climb Mount Kitchikoot

"I climb the mountain every Chinese New Year for chok dee." That's how my Thai friend, Nan, explained the reason for his upcoming trip to the chedi (shrine) of the Buddha's Footprint on Mount Kitchikoot. "You should come with me and get good luck, too." Three years previously he lived at the mountain shrine for six months, maintaining the site and assisting the pilgrims who came there. Since then, he returns each Chinese New Year for luck.

I'm a sailor, so I too believe strongly in luck. But uphill hiking through jungle is not among my favorite pastimes. Nan reassured me, " There is very little walking to do. We will take the midnight bus from Bangkok to Chantaburi and then a siilor (a covered pickup truck with bench seats) to Wat Phueng, a temple at the bottom of Khao Kitchikoot. From there, a big truck will take us far up the mountain so we have to walk only 45 minutes to the chedi."

While at sea, I know how to get luck from an albatross or a dolphin, on land, I'm all-adrift. But an hour and a half stroll seemed a fair exchange for chok dee, especially at this auspicious time of year. Still doubtful, I asked, "How do you know that you get good luck from this?" Nan answered, "Nothing bad has happened to me since I've been going there." Overwhelmed by such direct logic, my objections caved in. Besides, I might get lucky and take some good photos from the mountain top.

No such luck. We arrived in Chantaburi at 5 A.M. and boarded a siilor for the 20 mile ride to Wat Phueng. The day brightened to reveal a sodden countryside under a low overcast that drizzled all the way to Wat Phueng and completely obscured Mount Kitchikoot and the other tall peaks nearby. The driver said it had been raining hard for a week and this was a good day.

The temple of Wat Phueng glowed like an island of color in the mist of the gray morning. Its gold trim, blue tile roof, columns and doors inlaid with bits of colored glass stood in direct contrast to its drab surroundings where the comings and goings of vehicles had churned the temple grounds into a mud bog. Twenty empty busses clustered on the high ground like marooned animals, leaving the passengers to trudge like insects through honey, alternately sliding, skidding, and skating on the mud — out of control. The site looked like an overturned anthill as hundreds of people milled about. Several small groups sheltered under trees, and others collected around the noodle and coffee vendors' carts. A large, low cistern stood next to the temple, surrounded by people dipping into the water to wash the mud off themselves. After only a few steps my boots were encased in goo so I stopped at the cistern to clean them. There, the people looked at me curiously. Some nodded and smiled. The man next to me said, "You number one farang." But I don't know whether he meant the best foreigner or the only foreigner.

We joined a stream of people and boarded a large stake bed truck. When it's dry, the truck travels several miles up the rutted, mountain road. Today the ride ended in less than a mile. The steep track was so slippery that the truck sort of dog trotted sideways as far as it could and stopped. Nan told me that we now had to walk for about three hours to the shrine.

"Three hours? One way?" I asked, hoping he had made a mistake in word choice and really meant two, or even one-and-a-half. "Three hours go, three hours come back," he answered. With a couple of hours for rest time and visiting the shrine we would be on the trail for eight hours. My desire for good fortune was rapidly diminishing. I mean, why turn an inquisitive search for prosperity into a quest? I might get enough luck just by hanging around Wat Phueng for the day. Nan sensed my indecision and pretended to fuss with his day pack while I made up my mind.

I looked around. The empty truck had already left and my fellow passengers began moving. We looked like a mixed bag of riders on a Chinatown bus in Bangkok who had suddenly been transported through space to this soggy, mountain road. Most wore typical Bangkok street clothes — button shirts, long trousers, slacks and blouses. A group of teenagers decked out in designer jeans and flashy, sports shoes helped an elderly couple dressed in simple, collarless farmers' clothes and sandals. One thing was common to all. Everyone was going up the road. I can't turn back now, I thought, I'll lose face. I started up the road towards the clouds and Kitchikoot.

Before long, Nan had collected two more packs. He would carry them up the mountain for the owners. "Sometimes I would make three trips a day carrying bags for people, to gain merit." Our truckload of passengers had joined with the ones ahead to form a continuous line resembling a safari. Some wore backpacks, others clutched plastic shopping bags overflowing with incense and flowers. Nearly everyone had a walking staff. A half-mile up the road, the trail of people entered the jungle. "A shortcut," Nan assured me.

The tall trees and broad ferns of Kitchikoot's ancient forest formed a rainproof canopy above the narrow path. Corkscrew vines grew from twisted, half buried roots to ascend like petrified rope into the trees. In a small meadow, a low cloud crossed the trail and people disappeared as though into another dimension. Thai music floated past my ears when a group of teenagers overtook me; one of them carried a portable stereo on his shoulder. The path angled upwards and behind me I heard laughter and excited voices — someone had slipped and was sliding backwards on all fours, knocking people over. Ahead a jam-up formed as people clambered, hand-over-hand, through a web of roots, which had been exposed by the rain. Children chattered and scampered alongside the trail like squirrels

At mid-morning, we arrived at the halfway point, a large clearing around a shrine topped boulder and saffron swathed tree. This is an important spiritual site on the Kitchikoot pilgrimage and people bustled about lighting incense, pasting gold leaf to the shrine and conferring with the attending monks. On one side of the clearing a long roof sheltered the open-air mess hall where two huge cauldrons of rice porridge simmered on charcoal fires and boisterous diners filled tables and benches with lively chatter.

Near the path, people clustered around the coffee stalls, meeting with friends they hadn't seen since last year. Nan told me that devotees had been coming here for more than 10 years, as many as 1000 on a weekend. We had coffee with two of Nan's friends who lived at the Kitchikoot shrine and made merit by carrying bags for visitors. They had already made two trips to the top that day. Tired and muddy, they would make one more trip. Compared to them, my trek for luck was a piece of cake.

From here, the path climbed steeply to Kitchikoot ridge. It wound its way up a mountain side strewn with smooth, elephant sized boulders. Their random heaps formed niches and grottoes, the homes of spirits where passersby made offerings of incense, candles and fruit. On the ridge, the path widened and people congregated around the noodle stalls that lined one side. While others rested the in the overnight shelters on the other side. Down the middle, the line of marchers moved steadily towards the chedi a short distance up the ridge.

"There is the Luuk Baht." Nan pointed to a somewhat rounded boulder the size of a three-story house. This "Buddha's Alms Bowl," rested on a 30' long slab of rock that was covered with fresh flowers. This was the Phra Baht, the Buddha's Footprint where hundreds of worshipers burned thousands of joss sticks and the scented smoke was as thick as fog. After making our offerings we went to the nearby Pha Non, the cluster of sheds that make up the living quarters for the monks and boys who maintain the chedi. There, the center of attraction is a life-size statue of the Buddha holding an alms bowl. The smiling likeness beams down from its raised pedestal at the crowd circling below as they put coins into the monk's alms bowls that surrounded the base. Everyone tried to toss a coin into the luuk baht held by the statue. Nan explained that it was an especially good sign if the coin went into the bowl on the first try. My toss was good so I prepared myself for the best.

As I watched the rituals, a middle-aged monk approached and asked if I spoke English. He said that although he studied the language, he seldom had an opportunity to converse in it. I asked him about the theory of making merit and getting good luck. He explained, in a general way, the results of making merit and some of the ways it is done. " Climbing to this place today is an act of merit," he said. As for "good luck," he agreed that merit making was a good investment to improve one's fortunes, "But there are more immediate rewards to be enjoyed from making merit like this". I didn't ask him to name any since my dictionary was too small to deal with philosophy in detail.

The descent was as demanding on my legs as the climb up had been on my lungs. It was late afternoon and the overcast sky darkened prematurely; still, people were heading uphill. As they passed, some would ask the rhetorical question, "How far?" "Only a little farther," Nan rhetorically answered. Others took a break from their uphill climb and rested with us for awhile. During one of these stops I thought about what the monk had said, "immediate rewards."

Immediate? Right now? My legs felt like they were made by Michelin and I looked like I came out second best in a mud fight. These aren't the immediate rewards, are they? I looked up to see a young boy and an elderly woman coming up the trail, cautiously picking their way through the mud. He looked at me, smiled confidently and gave the "thumbs up" sign of friendship. "Chok Dee, good luck," I said. The old woman looked up and waved. There was my immediate reward. I was the only farang among a thousand Thai and Chinese and they had accepted, encouraged, and befriended me without question. What's more, they allowed me to share their spiritual experience on Mount Kitchikoot.

When we left Wat Phueng for Chantaburi the overcast had lifted so that the outline of Kitchikoot was visible. In the low light of dusk I looked back at the mountain and picked out tiny flickers of lights on its sides, the torches of those making the ascent. I wondered which one belonged to the old woman and boy. For me, my good luck had already begun — I made the trip in the daytime.

Notes

Bangkok Survivors Handbook and map -- $17.95
Shipping by Media Mail -- $2 in USA (5-7 days)
Shipping by Priority Mail -- $4.50 in USA (3-5 days)
Inquire about shipping costs outside of USA.

Your order will be shipped within 2 days

To order online

www.dreambuilderstv.com/bangkok/index.htm
Credit card payment accepted through Paypal.

To order by mail

Send the form below along with a check or money order for $17.95, plus shipping to:

Expat Publications
Robert Hein
6070 NE Emerson St.
Portland, OR 97218

Name _____

Address _____

City _____ State _____ Zip _____

Country _____

Email Address _____